POSTE RESTANTE

Poste Restante
A LAWRENCE
TRAVEL CALENDAR

HARRY T. MOORE

INTRODUCTION BY

MARK SCHORER

UNIVERSITY OF CALIFORNIA PRESS
Berkeley and Los Angeles 1956

University of California Press
Berkeley and Los Angeles, California

Cambridge University Press
London, England

Designed by Rita Carroll

Library of Congress Catalog Card No.: 56–8475

Printed in the United States of America

CONTENTS

PREFACE

Geography differs from biography, according to one of E. C. Bentley's clerihews, in that "geography is about maps" while "biography is about chaps." But sometimes the subjects intertwine, as they do in the career of D. H. Lawrence, whose travels are so important a part of his life and writings. The present book is his geographical biography.

He had once thought of permanent settlement, but toward the end of his life usually spoke of needing only a *pied à terre*, a temporary lodging. He often told his correspondents to address him in care of his agents, or *poste restante* at the next halting place. "We are going now to ———," he used to say: "Heaven knows why!" And the reference to heaven was more than bromidic. As Rebecca West once remarked, Lawrence's wanderings were like those of a Holy Man, whose journeys have a goal that is not really geographical but spiritual.

The record of Lawrence's travels is an organization of minor chronological facts—scattered thousands of them. A few years ago, when I started writing a long biography of Lawrence (*The Intelligent Heart*, published in 1955), I felt the need for a Calendar of his voyages and began constructing the one which appears here; indeed, it might serve as an appendix to *The Intelligent Heart*. Recently, the availability of some new material and a chance for a review of all the details of the Calendar have greatly expanded the original. It can now give a surprisingly complete account of Lawrence's daily whereabouts beginning with 1912. (From then on, his many letters provide us with most of the details, though sometimes their misdating can lead us astray.)

A Calendar of his travels should certainly be helpful to future biographers of Lawrence, as it was to me—perhaps more so to them, for they will bring to it fresh eyes and new ideas, and by then the subject itself will have expanded further, as it dynamically continues to do. The Calendar will also, I think, be of service to editors, critics, and bibliographers. Collectors may find it useful, too, for if they have undated Lawrence letters, the Calendar may help date them, particularly those with arrival or departure clues. And perhaps students will enjoy this Calendar if only in the attempt to pick it apart.

I have tried throughout to correct errors of fact in the Lawrence literature. For example, one of its principal printed sources, the Huxley edition of the *Letters*, is often inaccurate in its specifications. This is not said to disparage the editorship of Mr. Huxley and his associate in the project, Mrs. Enid Hilton; their assembling of those letters back in 1932 was a pioneering task, and many of the data now at hand were not available then. But before it is issued again the Huxley volume needs extensive reëditing.

Lawrence's letters have also appeared in other volumes— abundantly in such books as Ada Lawrence Clarke's *Early Life of D. H. Lawrence*, Mabel Dodge Luhan's *Lorenzo in Taos*, the Brewsters' *Letters and Reminiscences*, and Frieda Lawrence's *"Not I, But the Wind . . ."*; and occasionally in autobiographies such as those of Sir Edward Marsh, Knud Merrild, Curtis Brown, and others. About a thousand un-published letters went into the background work for this

Calendar; more than two hundred of these appear in *The Intelligent Heart*. A few of them came from my own collection, many of them from facsimiles in university libraries, and some from private collections. That Lawrence was a prolific correspondent no one has doubted; the miracle is that almost all the letters glow so brightly.

Sometimes their very spontaneity and brilliant hastiness make them difficult to use as counters for tabulation. Lawrence's dating of letters was often incomplete, occasionally wrong. He would of course have laughed at attempts to work them into a Calendar; but to do this has been fun, not only for the detective work it involved, but for the further acquaintance with Lawrence that it encouraged.

Through all the travels and all the writing of novels, poems, and essays, Lawrence kept his correspondence flowing. The parts of it as yet unpublished contain not only letters and postcards, but also the kind of notes everyone writes, the brief undated scrawls stuck in the mailboxes or slid under the doors of friends who were not at home. Lawrence left such scribbles for the Carswells, the Crosbys, Giuseppe Orioli; and almost alone among his writings, these lack his distinctive touch of language (small wonder, and no blame); yet even these bits sometimes provide useful information for the biographer or Calendar-maker. Lawrence rarely dated a postcard (except sometimes by the day of the week), but with cards the postmark is often a clue, if one remains and if it is decipherable. It may suggest the day of writing—or the day after, when it got into the mails. But, alas, there are times when even the harmless pursuit of stamp-collecting works against the scholar. The bright, exotic stamps on Lawrence's cards and letters were often important to the children of his friends. This accounts for the fantastic misdating of so much of the correspondence in

Ada Lawrence Clarke's *Early Life of D. H. Lawrence;* this sister of Lawrence's had given the stamps to her little boy, Jack, and when after Lawrence's death she tried to date the postcards for her book, she often guessed wrong by several years. The literary detective knows a sharp disappointment when his tired eyes look at the back of a postcard where he hopes to find a date across a stamp, and he can discover only a tiny square—blank except for some such legend as "Fabrication Suisse."

There were times when Lawrence seemed to believe in punctiliousness in the dating of letters. Consider what he wrote to Mrs. Hilton from the *vigie* on the Île de Port-Cros during his visit there in the autumn of 1928. Lawrence began his letter to Mrs. Hilton (as yet unpublished): "I got your letter only yesterday, saying you would be in Toulon. It wasn't dated either, so I don't know when you were there— probably last week, when I was all alone in Le Lavandou, and should have been so glad to see you!!" Now, Mrs. Hilton's failure to date a letter inspired Lawrence, who before and after this often dated his letters only "Wednesday" or "Saturday"—inspired him on this occasion to hammer down the date, "Sunday, 21 Oct 1928."

As we shall see, however, Lawrence was not always correct when he used all four elements of a date; indeed, his attempts at this method often need to be carefully checked. For the Calendar I have reëxamined all dates in the Lawrence letters concerned, particularly in the unpublished ones. As an example of a common type of error among these, consider the given data concerning Lawrence's arrival at the French-Riviera town of Bandol in September, 1929. One of his letters published in the Brewsters' memoir and dated "17 Sept. 1929," says: "We arrived Monday evening—three days ago." Something is wrong here, for the

17th of September, 1929, was a Tuesday. As for possible arrival at Bandol three days before the 17th, Lawrence was in Rottach-am-Tegernsee, Bavaria, on the 14th, as a letter in the Huxley collection shows. Further letters from there indicate that he was still in Rottach on the 15th and 16th. Also, an unpublished note to Charles Lahr, from Rottach on the 16th, mentions departure on "Wed."—or the 18th. But when did Lawrence arrive at Bandol? I have found (unpublished) two brief jottings from there on the 23rd, one to Caresse Crosby and one to Lahr. These were apparently written upon arrival. The one to Lahr suggests that the Lawrences had stopped over in Marseilles; and they may have spent a day or two somewhere else on that coast—evidence may turn up sometime to show this. In any event, the "23 Sept." of the Crosby-Lahr notes is certainly the "Monday evening" of the letter to Earl Brewster. That letter was probably written on the 27th—a Friday, and within reasonable range of the "Monday evening" of "three days ago." The misdating may not have been Lawrence's: Earl Brewster, in transcribing the letter, may have put down 17 for 27, or a printer may have set it wrong.

If the original of the letter ever turns up, it will probably show "27 Sept. 1929." Yet Lawrence could be extensively wrong, as we can see (to take only one example) in the case of a letter to Mrs. Huxley dated, in her husband's edition, "Tuesday, 16 April, 1928." Here is an example of Lawrence's being wrong when using all four elements of a date. April 16 was a Monday that year. In errors of this kind the safest assumption is that the day of the week would be correct. Lawrence in traveling through out-of-the-way lands, often beyond the range of printed calendars, would be more likely to know the day of the week than the date. This does not invariably prove to be true, though in general it does. The letters present a variety of such puzzles. All this is like detective work in that most of it is routine checking, with every now and then the rewards of discovery.

Among the raw materials of this activity, Lawrence's holograph letters are the most important primary source. Most of them are legible, for he wrote a neat hand. Copies of these letters, in photostat or on microfilm, are sometimes less easy to read. And typescripts are not always trustworthy. I have one set of them, for example, which has Lawrence staying at the Bean Rivage at Bandol rather than at the Beau Rivage. Printed letters are often unreliable, too, in such details: consider Lawrence's postcard to Catherine Carswell from Florence in 1919, which in the Huxley collection places Lawrence at a *pensione* called the Balestra. That this was really the Balestri is a tiny detail: since it is the multiplication of such errors that one objects to most, let us hope that the present book reduces rather than adds to the list of them. Oddly enough, it was an extremely untrustworthy volume, Ada Lawrence Clarke's, that helped me catch this last mistake. It had the name Balestri correct—as I found when I looked it up.

The closer we can get to Lawrence holographs, the nearer we get to complete accuracy. But, even in these, we can find still another type of error. Sometimes Lawrence puts down the wrong month or even the wrong year. The latter is the kind of mistake all of us are guilty of in the first days of a new year. An example from Lawrence is the letter published for the first time on p. 308 of *The Intelligent Heart*. Written to Jan Juta from a ranch on a remote shelf of the Rockies, it carries the date, "1 Jan. 1922"—a manifest impossibility, for Lawrence did not land in America for the first time until September 4, 1922. It was easy to make this correction in the book by putting the year 1923 in brackets after Lawrence's wrong date. And sometimes among his letters a similar kind of mistake crops up in the early days of a new month. A discussion of such an error occurs under the "about July 19" [1921] listing in the present Calendar. Lawrence could hardly have arrived at Thumersbach, Zell-am-See, Austria, before that day, yet a letter from there in the Huxley collection bears the date of July 7. The correct date is probably August 7, and perhaps the mistake was originally Lawrence's own rather than that of a transcriber or printer. Once again, this is a common type of error, particularly among those who have been traveling.

Sometimes Lawrence provides a good deal of plausible evidence for a single date of arrival or departure. When he has done this I have not usually crowded the Calendar with all the proof, but have tried to pick the references most readily accessible to the reader, particularly the Huxley collection, which so many libraries still have. Another consideration has been the fullness of each item concerned. If, for example, Lawrence on a certain day told one correspondent that he was leaving on the next day for Germany, that would be less important than a letter using almost the same language but naming the specific town in Germany to which he was going.

Lawrence's travel books are another source used for this Calendar. Three of the four of them record, with complete accuracy, day-to-day journeys: the walk across Switzerland in *Twilight in Italy,* the Sicilian and Italian and Sardinian travel in *Sea and Sardinia,* and the visits to the tomb cities of the Maremma in *Etruscan Places.* The fourth book in this category, *Mornings in Mexico,* is a series of loosely related sketches rather than a travel book in the usual sense, but even this volume provides some bits of evidence concerning one of Lawrence's almost entirely uncharted tours—that to the Hopi country of Arizona. The three Mediterranean travel books, however, have diurnal accounts of specific journeys and provide clues for tracing Lawrence's progress. With a minimum of outside reference, the time-table of those travels can be reconstructed.

Occasionally, the memoirs of Lawrence's friends furnish direct evidence or background information—occasionally. Various friends who visited Lawrence or accompanied him on tours are not mentioned in the Calendar, except in rare instances when necessity demanded their inclusion. The reader should remember that sometimes the "we" of the travels is Lawrence and one of his friends, not Lawrence and his wife, Frieda. On the Etruscan tour, for example, it is Earl Brewster whom necessity brings into the text. But the Calendar would be top heavy if it identified everyone at every way station. Nor are the sometimes separate travels of Frieda Lawrence, such as those of her visits to her family in Germany that Lawrence did not make with her, usually mentioned. Occasionally, Lawrence wove references to her separate travels closely into his own necessary geographical narratives, and then the reader will see that Frieda is away or is going away or is returning; but this kind of notation does not occur throughout. Her comings and goings are fairly easy to trace in previously published material. Here, the focus had to be on Lawrence exclusively. He is the protagonist of the little drama of this Calendar.

In regard to Lawrencean geography, the Calendar is fairly detailed. The date-entries include current address, route, name of steamship or railway lines, whenever these are known—even county or province. Some readers may not find these last items strictly necessary, but those following the subject closely will welcome such details for quick location of out-of-the-way places. Often the date-entry will repeat all the particulars of address in order to save the reader the trouble of looking back and checking these data from the last time Lawrence stayed at that place. Most of this referential detail (of address or name of steamship) the Calendar presents without naming its origin, even when the material is from an unpublished source, inaccessible to the reader. There is simply not room for everything here. In quoting from Lawrence's letters, published or unpublished, I have for use in the Calendar almost always pinched off the necessary phrase or sentence that identified the geography and have let everything else go—with regret, often with sharp regret. For always beyond the locality-tag a fresh landscape or seascape stretched, vibrating through Lawrence's prose as the fair places of the earth vibrate before us. Yet even the cataloguing of the Lawrencean places will project living pictures of them to those who know Lawrence's writings.

The Calendar for the sake of exactness presents all the geographical data without abbreviation. But to save space it shortens some of the bibliographical references, as the table of abbreviations (immediately preceding the Calendar) shows. In devising the abbreviations I sometimes put them into two initials, sometimes into three. For most of the books concerned, the names of the authors seemed more appropriate as abbreviations than the names of their books. The initials AH, for example, stand for Aldous Huxley's edition of *The Letters of D. H. Lawrence,* BYN for Witter Bynner's *Journey With Genius,* CC for Catherine Carswell's *The Savage Pilgrimage,* and so on. Admittedly, the abbreviations are not consistent, but a rigid system would have produced conflicts. For Lawrence's own books, I have used what seemed to be the key initials of their titles. In any event, the abbreviations are both few and simple; anyone using the Calendar should very soon become familiar with them. The books listed opposite these abbreviations have the date and place not of their first editions, but of the editions most accessible, at this writing, to American readers. When the English pagination duplicates that of one of these American editions, I have noted it also. When there is no American edition, as with Ada Lawrence Clarke's *Early Life of D. H. Lawrence*, the British publication only is noted: in this particular case, the English printing is certainly more accessible in both England and America than the earlier Florentine edition.

The Calendar is essentially for the use and even for the entertainment of students of Lawrence and of contemporary literature in general. To some strangers to Lawrence it may look the way an elaborate problem in differential calculus looks to the non-mathematician. But perhaps, as occasionally happens with puzzles, some newcomers to the subject who discover this Calendar will, as part of an attempt to find their way about in it, begin to read Lawrence. That is to be hoped for.

Harry T. Moore

Wellesley Hills, Mass.
March 2, 1956

ACKNOWLEDGMENTS

My first thanks go to Mr. Mark Schorer, who followed up his initial interest in the Lawrence Calendar by writing the Introduction to this book. I am also most grateful to Mr. William A. Jackson, Director of the Houghton Library of Harvard University; to Mr. Gene Magner, Curator of the Modern Poetry Collection of the Lockwood Memorial Library of the University of Buffalo; and to Mr. J. Terry Bender, Curator of the Division of Special Collections of the Stanford University Libraries; all of them have kindly lent Lawrence materials in their possession. And Mr. John Carswell has generously let me use more than a hundred unpublished letters to his mother from Lawrence. Several collectors and other individuals interested in Lawrence have kindly sent me important data: Mr. Jewell Stevens, Mr. George S. Lazarus, Mr. Roger W. Straus, Jr., and Mr. Edward Nehls. Mr. Nehls, who is preparing a huge collection of published and unpublished memoirs of Lawrence, has been most generous in sharing documents and information. For permission to quote from published and unpublished Lawrence letters I am once again indebted to Mrs. Frieda Lawrence Ravagli, to Mr. Laurence Pollinger, and to the Viking Press, which holds American publication rights to all Lawrence letters. Also, I am again grateful for the moral and editorial assistance of my wife, who has been exceedingly patient through all the weathers of preparing six Lawrence books—of which series we both hope that the present volume will be the last.

H.T.M.

INTRODUCTION

BY MARK SCHORER

Poste restante!
So any knowing correspondent would have labeled the
envelope of almost any letter he was addressing to D. H.
Lawrence. *Poste restante,* or *Post-lagernd,* or *Hold until
called for*—a half dozen languages, a dozen countries, but
always the same admonition. How many postal clerks the
world over must have observed it, wondered briefly or not
wondered about the identity of the English mister, at last
looked him in the face as they handed him his packet of
accumulated mail, and then, once having seen this improb-
able addressee, thin and red and dusty and vivid, wondered
about him indeed! Certainly the admonition on his letters
was indispensable if the mail was by any chance to reach
him. A paraphrased refrain of Lawrence's correspondence
runs like this: *We are here . . . We leave tomorrow, write
me at . . . Everything changed, we are still here . . . Tomorrow we may be off after all . . . We are still here . . .
We are off at last, and in two days will be at . . . We have
come here instead . . . We are leaving, I will send address.*

The most casual leafing through of Lawrence's letters, the
unpublished together with the published, invokes at once

a sense of the relentlessness of his itinerant life, and ten different leafings through would produce ten catalogues of travel in general like the following, each different from the others only as to details of place. In 1918 Lawrence wrote from England, "Frieda is pretty well—wondering what is to become of us. There are primroses in the wood and avenues of yellow hazel catkins, hanging like curtains." In 1920, from Taormina: "At the moment I feel I never want to see England again—if I move, then further off, further off"; a few months later, from the Abruzzi: "I feel all unstuck, as if I might drift anywhere"; and eighteen months after that, from Taormina again, "Our great news is that we are going to Ceylon." Ceylon promptly proved unsatisfactory: "Here we are on a ship again—somewhere in a very big blue choppy sea with flying fishes sprinting out of the waves like winged drops, and a Catholic Spanish priest playing Chopin at the piano—very well—and the boat gently rolling . . . We are going to Australia—Heaven knows why . . ." Less than six months later, from Taos, New Mexico: "We got here last week and since then I have been away motoring for five days into the Apache country to see an Apache dance. It is a weird country, and I feel a great stranger still." The stay in New Mexico and Mexico was to be long enough to make of these places as much a home for Lawrence as any he was to know after his native Nottinghamshire, and yet, in 1924, inevitably, he writes: "We are packing up to leave here on Saturday . . . It is time to go." England again, and then, in late 1925, from Spotorno, south of Genoa, "We got here yesterday—it's lovely and sunny, with a blue sea, and I'm sitting out on the balcony just above the sands, to write. Switzerland was horrid—I don't like Switzerland anyhow—in slow rain and snow. We shall find ourselves a villa here, I think, for the time." The time was short, as usual, and presently they were living outside Florence, and from there, in 1927, he wrote: "I have put off coming to England. I just feel I don't want to come north—feel a sort of migration instinct pushing me south rather than north." But in the next year he wrote to Harry Crosby from Switzerland, "I suppose we shall stay a week or two, then perhaps move up the mountain a little higher—my woful [*sic*] bronchials! How are you and where are you and where are you going?" From the south of France less than a year before his death, Lawrence could still write, "I wonder where we shall ultimately settle! At the moment I feel very undecided about everything. I shall send an address as soon as I have one." And then in 1929 he had one, the last: "We have got this little house on the sea for six months, so the address is good. It is a rocky sea, very blue, with little islands way out, and mountains behind Toulon—still a touch of Homer, in the dawn—we like it—& it is good for my health . . ." But in less than six months the long, circling journey was over.

This odyssey that only death could end, as uneasy as it was adventurous, of the most restless spirit in a world that seems more stable than it is because his restlessness strides and flashes and flies across it—this odyssey, if we are to see it in its multiple and shifting details, demands an itinerary that is fixed at last in print; Lawrence's, more than any other modern literary life, should have a calendar.

The chief reason for this necessity is that all the time that Lawrence was moving, he was also writing, and the settings of his works follow upon the march of his feet. It is in no way surprising, of course, that a writer, and especially a novelist, should assimilate his travels in his works; but there is probably no other writer in literary history whose works responded so immediately to his geographical environment as Lawrence, and certainly there is no other modern writer to whose imagination "place" made such a direct and intense appeal, and in whose works, as a consequence, place usurps such a central role. Often it becomes the major character, as it were, Lawrence's arbiter, disposing of human destinies in accordance with the response that the human characters have made to itself, the non-human place. Or one may say that Lawrence's people discover their identities through their response to place, and that, having thus come upon their true selves, they mark out their fate and are able to pursue it to another place—factory or farm, city or country, north or south, England or Italy, Europe or America, death or life.

This catalogue of polarities should suggest what is in fact the one basic polarity that motivated Lawrence's attitude toward place and his use of it in his fiction. It was a polarity in which, as a child and a boy and a young man, his vision was daily educated, on which his imagination was forced to feed, and which finally formed the core of his intellectual view. It is a polarity that founds itself on the distinction between natural place and natural place corrupted by unnatural circumstance. The early forms of the distinction are literal and simple: from his childhood on, landscape and the country were freedom, the industrial town and the city were mechanical slavery. An early novel like *Sons and Lovers* may be said to base its drama on values symbolized by the contradiction between flowers growing in the sunny fields and woods, and men working in the black depths of coal mines. In *The Intelligent Heart*, Mr. Moore tells us that as a young school teacher Lawrence found only drawing and "nature study" congenial to him. The botanizing impulse throughout his poetry is evident from the start, and his novels from the beginning tended to organize themselves around the poles of place—civilized and wild, city and farm, mine and field. Industrialism, "the base forcing of human energy," almost inevitably made geography the first symbolic statement in anything he wrote, as, likewise, it was to drive him to the remote places of the world. War, the dehumanizing process of society in the destructive mass, always seemed to him a portion of the industrial process, and it is not accidental that Lawrence's hatred of industrial England seems to have reached its height during the war years when, in a letter to Catherine Carswell, he wrote, "I can't live in England. I can't stop any more. I shall die of foul inward poison. The vital atmosphere of the country is poisonous to an incredible degree: to me at least. I shall die in the fumes of their stench. But I *must* get out."

Thus, a polarity that began at the level of visual observation of place grows in the imagination into the difference between entities no smaller than war and peace themselves, and thus "place" can become a major symbol of distinction and judgment in Lawrence's great and sustained concern with "that sacrifice of life to circumstance which I most strongly disbelieve in." It was this sacrifice that made Lawrence sometimes rage in his work as it made him wander in his life, and there is merit in Mr. Moore's argument that there was an impersonality in this rage, that he was "a channel of rage . . . on behalf of life and growth." Lawrence himself said, "*I* won't have another war . . . I am not one man, I am many, I am most." Alas!

At the outset, then, England provided the still coupled poles of place, and the earliest work invokes a kind of dream of an older England that is dying as it paints a dark picture of the new England that is death itself. The opening paragraph of Lawrence's first, and very young novel, *The White Peacock*, strikes the note:

I stood watching the shadowy fish slide through the gloom of the mill-pond. They were grey, descendants of the silvery things that had darted away from the monks, in the young days when the valley was lusty. The whole place was gathered in the musing of old age. The thick-piled trees on the far shore were too dark and sober to dally with the sun; the weeds stood crowded and motionless. Not even a little wind flickered the willows of the islets. The water lay softly, intensely still. Only the thin stream falling through the mill-race murmured to itself of the tumult of life which had once quickened the valley.

Lawrence's insights are still unanalyzed in this novel that is without any formal focus, and yet the suggestion seems clearly there in the picture of the ruined feudal farm, Strelley Mill overrun by rabbits, and in the picture of Annable, who has turned his back on society and lives by choice in primitive squalor, that the fault lies in civilization, that with the invasions of an industrial way of life and the end of that great, slow cultural convulsion which was the Industrial Revolution, human responses have split into warring dualities and have thinned out, sound human passions have been enervated as natural place has been devastated and corrupted. In his next novel, *The Trespasser*, Lawrence presents two victims of these warring and debilitated responses and shows them fleeing from the dark city to the Isle of Wight, where, wrapped in the hot mists of the island, they make the belated attempt to heal themselves in a feverish, Wagnerian debauch that can only drive the war deeper and that kills one of them. This is a poor novel, but the major importance of the island to its structure as to its meaning foreshadows a major characteristic of the novels that are to come. It is in the next, *Sons and Lovers*, that Lawrence seems to push his initial intuition about place and the opposition of kinds of place into their full cultural and psychological implications. His profound response to the natural world and his deep loathing for the unnatural things that are done to it now become articulate in this novel that opposes flower and farm and field to mine and machine and factory, creativeness and growth to mechanization and death, men and women struggling to live in wholeness to men and women determined to die in division.

It is in *Sons and Lovers,* appropriately, that we become aware of that element at the very heart of Lawrence's genius, the ability to convey the unique quality of physical experience that is so central to his power of communicating the spirit of places. This ability shows best in Lawrence's descriptions of non-human things, in his writing of animals, flowers and grass, fish, birds, snakes—a genius for identifying and defining the individuated quality of life, the physical essences of things outside the personality, the not-me, the very *ding an sich.* Some of Lawrence's poems, notably those in the volume called *Birds, Beasts, and Flowers,* reveal this ability in its most intense purity, but we see it flashing all through *Sons and Lovers,* in every natural description, and we begin to see how it will come to form the basis of Lawrence's sense of individual integrity and human relationships. At one point in the novel, when Paul Morel is sketching, Miriam asks, "Why do I like this so?"

"Why *do* you?" he asked.
"I don't know. It seems so true."
"It's because—it's because there is scarcely any shadow in it; it's more shimmery, as if I'd painted the shimmering protoplasm in the leaves and everywhere, and not the stiffness of the shape. That seems dead to me. Only this shimmeriness is the real living. The shape is a dead crust. The shimmer is inside reality."

The "shimmer," the "inside reality" in human individuals and relationships, in love no less than in place and natural

forms, Lawrence pursued above all else, and he was implying now and would soon enough demonstrate explicitly, that
the several varieties of reality are deeply interdependent.
The corruptions of place and the corruptions of men are a
single process, and with these corruptions, the "inside reality" is itself destroyed as place and men yield to the mechanical form, the "husk." Husks, chiefly, Lawrence be-
lieved, were modern men, deprived of vital connections
with life outside themselves, ensnared in their partial and
divisive and mechanized "personalities." To discover a place
where the vital connections could be maintained intact was
the motive of Lawrence's life as it increasingly becomes the
motive of his heroes and heroines.

Before he had finished the final version of *Sons and
Lovers,* Lawrence was already traveling and living outside
England: the icy blue mountains and the black firs of Germany, the north, help to create the extraordinary, destructive atmosphere of an early story like "The Prussian Officer,"
and the lemon yellow air of the south, the sharp and yet
somehow dreaming pathos of the first travel sketches in
Twilight in Italy. In short, Lawrence had already started
what was to grow into his vast and vastly various com-
pendium of impressions, whether in essay, poem, story, or
novel, of places all over the world, continuously supple-
mented until the very end of his life, and always written
with his unique freshness and dash. But he was not yet,
nor would he ever quite be finished with England and the
primary poles of place, together with their poles of value,
that England meant to him.

The next novel, *The Rainbow,* is a slow and careful writing out of the whole long process of the transformation of
the old England into the new, and a dramatization of the
concomitant alteration in human functions. Perhaps no

single passage in Lawrence communicates more fully his sense of the relation of place and character than that idyllic opening description of the old yeoman way of life in Britain:

The Brangwens had lived for generations on the Marsh Farm, in the meadows where the Erewash twisted sluggishly through alder trees, separating Derbyshire from Nottinghamshire. Two miles away, a church-tower stood on a hill, the houses of the little country town climbing assiduously up to it. Whenever one of the Brangwens in the fields lifted his head from his work, he saw the church-tower at Ilkeston in the empty sky. So that as he turned again to the horizontal land, he was aware of something standing above him and beyond him in the distance. . . . They felt the rush of the sap in spring, they knew the wave which cannot halt, but every year throws forward the seed to begetting, and, falling back, leaves the young-born on the earth. They knew the intercourse between heaven and earth, sunshine drawn into the breast and bowels, the rain sucked up in the daytime, nakedness that comes under the wind in autumn, showing the birds' nests no longer worth hiding. Their life and inter-relations were such; feeling the pulse and body of the soil, that opened to their furrow for the grain, and became smooth and supple after their ploughing, and clung to their feet with a weight that pulled like desire, lying hard and unresponsive when the crops were to be shorn away. The young corn waved and was silken, and the lustre slid along the limbs of the men who saw it. They took the udder of the cows, the cows yielded milk and pulse against the hands of the men, the pulse of the blood of the teats of the cows beat into the pulse of the men. They mounted their horses, and held life between the grip of their knees, they harnessed their horses at the wagon, and, with hand on the bridle-rings, drew the heaving of the horses after their will.

From this initial condition of natural harmony between man and his environment, the novel traces the disintegration of both men and the environment, the dissolution of harmony, the frenetic disintegration of life, and concludes with a visionary challenge to new integration under still other circumstances of place, yet to come. In *Women in Love*, a kind of sequel, we observe two couples who are concerned to achieve the new integration: one couple achieves it, the other does not, but the solution no longer lies within England itself. In this novel, England has become the full symbol of mechanization, and it is the Continent that is opposed to it. On the Continent, the poles of place once more become the north and the south, the icy Alps and the golden Italian reaches of hill and flowering plain and Renaissance city below.

> . . . as by a miracle she remembered that away beyond, below her, lay the dark fruitful earth, that towards the south there were stretches of land dark with orange trees and cypress, grey with olives, that ilex trees lifted wonderful plumy tufts in shadow against a blue sky. Miracle of miracles!—this utterly silent, frozen world of the mountain-tops was not universal! One might leave it and have done with it. One might go away.

One might go away! The theme of the life as of the works. For two years now, while the Lawrences roamed the Italian cities with their *pied à terre* a farm house clinging to the hills over the sea at the edge of Taormina, Lawrence wrote two more novels that played their variations on the theme. In *The Lost Girl,* the heroine escapes the respectable stultifications of commercialized Nottinghamshire by following an Italian peasant into the hard life of the Abruzzi. The hero of *Aaron's Rod* leaves England for wanderings in Italy that are based on Lawrence's own, seeking his fulfillment in place, and the work is nearly as much travel book as it is novel. In the same period, Lawrence produced his second genuine travel book, *Sea and Sardinia.* As in *Twilight in Italy* he had seen industrial mechanization overcoming feudal Italy, so in his study of the vividly dark island, so long isolated from the culture of continental Europe, he sees Sardinia after it has been drawn into the despoiling tensions of continental war. Place, in Lawrence's account, is seldom presented without its cultural and even sociological implications as Lawrence perceives them, and these support his vivid descriptive gifts with an informal intellectual dimension that, even when, as in *Sea and Sardinia,* he is writing with extreme casualness, gives them a permanent seriousness. Or, if the implications are not directly cultural and sociological, they are psychological, as in that most intense evocation of all the places that he drew, the Sicilian landscape in the story, "Sun," in which, through the sustained pressure of an almost ferocious sensuosity, ritualistic rebirth is nearly accomplished; and accomplished through the power of place.

Aaron's Rod was a novel with political overtones: wandering through Italy, Aaron is also looking for a spiritual leader to whom he can submit his wounded individuality and be healed. Place becomes the political arena, and as, now, the Lawrencean wanderings themselves are flung out over wider areas in the world, travel and the search for spiritual rest are explicitly equated, in the work as in the life. The Australian novel, *Kangaroo,* which follows on the Sicilian period, is a novel of ideas that debates political alternatives for its Lawrencean hero, Lovat Somers. On the raw edge of the world, at once sordid and primitive, corrupt in its abrupt modernity and at the same time inspiring in its continuity with a past forever unawakened, Australia is both exhilarating and terrifying to its hero, as Lawrence makes it to us. The actualization of the dark spirit of this continent on the underside of the world is as solid as the psychological and political judgments are ambiguous, and the spiritually reductive terrors of the one together with the elusive emotional and intellectual demands of the other give Somers no opportunity for genuine choice. He abandons both Australia and the socialist-fascist alternative, and, like Lawrence, leaves for America, where he hopes to find a less disturbing place and a more plausible choice. "One walks away to another place," Lawrence had written to Aldous Huxley seven or eight years earlier, "and life begins anew." And he had added—ominously, prophetically— "But it is a midge's life."

In the New Mexico–Mexico period that follows, the landscape and the cultures and the place-spirit all change, but the pattern of the work remains constant. In his third travel book, *Mornings in Mexico,* Lawrence gives us again his most explicit understanding of the full quality of the new world that absorbs him. In the fiction, place as such becomes more powerful than it has ever been as the arbiter of human fortunes. *St. Mawr* is the story of two English-women, a mother and a daughter, who come to New Mexico to discover a life that will free them from the frustrating triviality of their social past, and in the end the daughter submits to the wild landscape itself, beyond humanity.

There's something else for me, mother. There's something else even that loves me and wants me. I can't tell you what it is. It's a spirit. And it's here, on this ranch. It's here, in this landscape. It's something more real to me than men are, and it soothes me, and it holds me up. I don't know what it is, definitely. It's something wild, that will hurt me sometimes and will wear me down sometimes. I know it. But it's something big, bigger than men, bigger than people, bigger than religion. It's something to do with wild America. And it's something to do with me. It's a mission, if you like. I am imbecile enough for that!—But it's my mission to keep myself for the spirit that is wild, and has waited so long here: even waited for such as me. Now I've come! Now I'm here. Now I am where I want to be: with the spirit that wants me.—And that's how it is.

In the cruelly beautiful novelette, "The Princess," a frozen New England virgin makes a ritual journey, half-fearful, half-wishful, over New Mexican mountains, the symbolic barriers, to her destruction. In "The Woman Who Rode Away," which is a fable rather than a story and the center of which is, literally now, a ritual of sacrifice, a woman yields up her consciousness with her life to the consciousness and the life of the Indians whose religion is continuous with the spirit of the place to which she has come. In each, place triumphs.

The Plumed Serpent, the most ambitious work of this period, alters this pattern in some degree. Nowhere in the length and breadth of his work does Lawrence's prose communicate more fully or more glamorously the physical character of his setting, in all its rich singularity, than in this long novel, yet in the end, in part at least, the human will is more powerful than the spirit of the place. Once more the story concerns a European woman in search of her soul. Lawrence himself is still involved in the political ideas of the great leader that had occupied him in two previous novels. In the atmosphere of Mexican political life, these ideas find a more plausible embodiment than they have previously had, and the attempt of Lawrence's two leaders to replace the imposed Christian god and the Christian saints with the primitive Aztec gods, and to work this effort into the fabric of a larger political program, hardly seems fantastic. But for the European woman, Kate Leslie, as finally, for Lawrence, the solution is no solution at all. For that place and for those people who are native to it, some such challenge to the corruptions of Western civilization may be inevitable and even right; but it will solve nothing for the woman from Ireland, even less for the searching miner's son from Nottinghamshire. The future of Kate Leslie is not clear, either in place or time. For Lawrence, the future is clearly not in politics; he will settle for "tenderness," for the individual human relationship, for that whole lovely freedom in self-responsible conduct that was included in his sense of the word *insouciance,* a word he came to love above most others. And so—"It is time to go."

The circle nearly closes. It is time to go to Nottinghamshire. Two books come out of this otherwise ill-fated return. The first, *The Virgin and the Gypsy,* a kind of trial-run for the other, *Lady Chatterley's Lover,* sweeps out the old England with a flood, and gives the virgin life on the crest of it. It is a simple and unfinished story published posthumously, and it is not very interesting apart from the final novel, in which the whole judgment on England is at last delivered. The judgment is not very different from, only more maddened than the judgment that was delivered in such an earlier novel as *Women in Love* or in such an elegy upon a dead culture as the story, "England, My England." We are back at the primary, coupled poles as, in *Lady Chatterley's Lover,* they are presented together again, coupled, the fulfilling and the destroying place; and the organization of place-value is now so close and so taut that we remember this novel as we remember a picture: in the background black machinery looms cruelly against a dark sky; in the foreground, hemmed in but brilliantly fresh, stands a green wood; in a clearing of the wood, two naked human beings dance.

There was no place in England where Lawrence could dance, no place there, in fact, where he could breathe. No patterned circle closes upon him! The last writing was done in Italy, at the Villa Mirenda, a farmhouse outside Florence. There were not many places where even a simple insouciance was possible, but this was one where it was.

Class makes a gulf, across which all the best human flow is lost. It is not exactly the triumph of the middle classes that has made

the deadness, but the triumph of the middle-class *thing*. . . .
the middle class is broad and shallow and passionless. Quite
passionless. At the best they substitute affection, which is the
great middle-class positive emotion. . . . Yet I find, here in
Italy, for example, that I live in a certain silent contact with the
peasants who work the land of this villa. I am not intimate with
them . . . and they are not working for me; I am not their
padrone. Yet it is they, really, who form my *ambiente* . . . I
don't expect them to make any millennium here on earth, neither
now nor in the future. But I want to live near them, because
their life still flows.

And his did. There at the Mirenda, Frieda Lawrence recalls, Lawrence would go every morning into the nearby
woods, settle himself next to a spring where San Eusebio
once meditated, look at the flowers and the birds at his
feet, and remember that other place, England, while he
wrote.

At the very end, he took this world of places that he had
known into another world where the implications of "place"
become more general than those immediately of this world.
The Man Who Died is a fable of the resurrection; it is set
in a hot Mediterranean country; the spirit becomes flesh, is
connected with the beauties and pressures of place, as of
society and of sex. Yet it is a fable—in the major sense, set
in a place out of this world. *Etruscan Places*, which may
be called the last of the travel books, is a re-creation in
Lawrence's terms of an ideal society, colorful and brave
and creative and, above all, insouciant. Stimulated by the
wonderfully vivid paintings in tombs such as those at Tarquinia, Lawrence created in his Etruscan "place" the most
living of all the societies that he had drawn. And the
Etruscans, Lawrence discovered, put a little bronze ship
of death on the tomb of their dead, symbol of the vessel
that would carry them on further travels. And now mines
disappear, machines disappear, science disappears, England

disappears: only wind and sea and sails remain. Only that
which is finally natural, only one last place . . .

> Now it is autumn and the falling fruit
> and the long journey towards oblivion.
>
> The apples falling like great drops of dew
> to bruise themselves an exit from themselves.
>
> And it is time to go, to bid farewell
> to one's own self, and find an exit
> from the fallen self.
>
> Have you built your ship of death, O have you?
> O build your ship of death, for you will need it.

How curious! And how to explain it, Lawrence's restlessness, if one had the temerity! In the last year of his life,
he wrote to the Richard Aldingtons in the old, perpetual
vein:

. . . in the late autumn, let's really go somewhere. Would you
go to Egypt if we went? We might find some way of doing it
cheap—& there *are* quite nice modest pensions in Cairo. Let's
go to Egypt in November, en quatre—& go sometimes & see
the Dobrees, & go up the Nile and look at the desert and perhaps
get shot in Khartoum like General Gordon.—Frieda of course,
woman-like, pines for more islands—Majorca & Minorca—but
I'm not keen on islands. The other thing is the Mediterranean
shore of Spain. I'd like to go to Madrid to the Prado. But I
don't want to stay in the Mirenda this winter. . . . Have you
got lots of flowers, beans & carrots. We have phlox in a tiny
fenced garden, & salad & a few turnips & red currants.

And only a month or two before his death he wrote to the
Huxleys from that last villa, less than a *pied à terre,* "Beau
Soleil" at Bandol,

I am thankful for this unredeemedly modern and small Beau
Soleil, taken for 6 months and no more, and am thankful to God

to escape anything like a permanency. "Better fifty years of Europe than a cycle of Cathay." Well, I've had nearly fifty years of Europe, so I should rather try the cycle of Cathay.

The question forces itself: what, up to the bitter black end, impelled him? But no answer comes; it lies in the still undefined history and character of our times.

There were superficial motives, of course. First, and for a long time, Lawrence moved about because he was continually looking for a place where he might conceivably establish that ideal community, Rananim, as it was to be called, for which he yearned over many years, that pre-Jeffersonian community of congenial and creative and co-operative persons (many were called but few chose) who would make their own society, outside the destructive pressures of society at large. Second, Lawrence moved because of his health—first south, then north; to the desert, then up into the mountains—always hoping for a climate in which his bleeding lungs would heal, even while he defied medical opinion and chose the place where he thought that his spirit might find rest.

I've been in bed this last week with bronchial haemorrhages—due, radically, to chagrin—though I was born bronchial—born in chagrin, too. But I'm better—shaky—shaky—and we're going to Austria tomorrow, D.V.—whoever D. may be—to the mountains.

. . . Well here we are—got through on Thursday night in the wagon-lit—not too tired and no bad consequences. I feel already much better. What with cool air, *a cool bed*, cool mountain water—it's like a new life. I never *would* have got well, down there in that heat in Tuscany. . . . It is such a mercy to be able to breathe and move. I take little walks to the country—and we sit by the river—the Drave—in the little town, under the clipped trees, very 18th-century German—Werther period. The river comes from the ice, and is very full and swift and pale and silent. It rather fascinates me . . .

And third, he moved about because he had an inexhaustible belief that somewhere a place would present itself that was in every way better than any other place he had known. In his writing, this place is finally discovered to be outside society but it is conceived in all of the most glowing colors of the natural world. Yet the last sentence of his last letter dies with his breath: "This place no good." It was time to move again.

He found no place where he could stay for long. But how much more beautiful and exciting and desirable, because of his vividly hopeful explorations of it, is this place where all the rest of us still are!

ACKNOWLEDGMENTS

I am indebted to several publishers for their coöperation. Excerpts from D. H. Lawrence's letters are published with the kind permission of The Viking Press, holders of publication rights to all the Lawrence letters. Viking has also permitted me to quote from *Sons and Lovers, Women in Love,* and *The Rainbow.* Curtis Brown Ltd. has permitted me to quote from *The White Peacock.* Alfred A. Knopf, Inc. has permitted me to quote from *St. Mawr* and *Assorted Articles,* both of which are included in *The Later D. H. Lawrence, the Best Novels, Stories, and Essays,* 1925 to 1930.

M. S.

ABBREVIATIONS

AH   Aldous Huxley, ed. *The Letters of D. H. Lawrence* (New York, The Viking Press, Inc., 1932)

ALC   Ada Lawrence (Clarke) [and G. Stuart Gelder], *Early Life of D. H. Lawrence* (London, Martin Secker, 1932)

BR   Earl and Achsah Brewster, *D. H. Lawrence: Reminiscences and Correspondence* (London, Martin Secker, 1934)

BYN   Witter Bynner, *Journey With Genius* (New York, The John Day Co., 1951)

CA   Lady Cynthia Asquith, *Remember and be Glad* (New York, Charles Scribner's Sons; London, James Barrie, 1952)

CC   Catherine Carswell, *The Savage Pilgrimage* (London, Chatto and Windus; New York, Harcourt, Brace & Co., 1932)

EM   Sir Edward Marsh, *A Number of People* (New York, Harper & Brothers, 1939)

FR   Frieda Lawrence, *"Not I, But the Wind. . . ."* (New York, The Viking Press, Inc., 1934)

HM   Harry T. Moore, *The Intelligent Heart: The Story of D. H. Lawrence* (New York, Farrar, Straus & Young, Inc.; London, William Heinemann, Ltd., 1955)

JC   (Jessie Chambers) E. T., *D. H. Lawrence: A Personal Record* (London, Jonathan Cape, 1935; New York, Knight Publications, 1936)

LKM   *The Letters of Katherine Mansfield* (New York, Alfred A. Knopf, Inc., 1929)

MER   Knud Merrild, *A Poet and Two Painters* (London, Routledge & Kegan Paul, 1938; New York, The Viking Press, Inc., 1939)

ML   Mabel Dodge Luhan, *Lorenzo in Taos* (New York, Alfred A. Knopf, Inc., 1932)

MTM   Katherine Mansfield's *Letters to John Middleton Murry* (London, Constable; New York, Alfred A. Knopf, Inc., 1951)

MXR   "The Unpublished Letters of D. H. Lawrence to Max Mohr," in *T'ien Hsai Monthly* (Shanghai, August and September, 1935). Pages referred to are those occupied by these letters in No's. 1 and 2 of Vol. 1 (pp. 21–36 and 166–179 of Vol. 1).

RA   Richard Aldington, *D. H. Lawrence: Portrait of a Genius But . . .* (New York, Duell, Sloan & Pearce, Inc., 1950)

RMM   John Middleton Murry, *Reminiscences of D. H. Lawrence* (New York, Henry Holt & Co., Inc., 1933)

RSL   *D. H. Lawrence's Letters to Bertrand Russell* (New York, Gotham Book Mart, 1948)

SFD   S. Foster Damon, *Amy Lowell: A Chronicle* (New York, Houghton Mifflin Co., 1935)

TPY   Caresse Crosby, *The Passionate Years* (New York, Dial Press, 1953)

BOOKS BY D. H. LAWRENCE

EP   *Etruscan Places* (London, William Heinemann, Ltd., New York, The Viking Press, Inc., 1933)

LAH   *Love Among the Haystacks* (New York, The Viking Press, Inc., 1933)

LDN   Diary Notes in *The Frieda Lawrence Collection of D. H. Lawrence Manuscripts* (Albuquerque, University of New Mexico Press, 1948). Pages referred to are those occupied by the Lawrence Diary Notes in the pages of this book (i.e., from p. 89 to p. 99).

LL   *The Later D. H. Lawrence* (New York, Alfred A. Knopf, Inc., 1952)

MIM   *Mornings in Mexico* (New York, Alfred A. Knopf, Inc., 1927)

PHX   *Phoenix* (New York, The Viking Press, Inc., 1936)

SRD   *Sea and Sardinia* (New York, Doubleday & Company, Inc., 1954)

TWI   *Twilight in Italy* (London, William Heinemann, Ltd., 1950)

THE TRAVEL CALENDAR

1885

SEPTEMBER 11. D. H. LAWRENCE BORN AT EASTWOOD, NOTTINGHAMSHIRE, ENGLAND

D. H. Lawrence's journey through life began on September 11, 1885: the facts underlying this metaphor were noted down on October 20 of that year by T. M. Nisc, then Registrar for the District of Basford, Nottinghamshire. The boy's parents were Arthur John Lawrence and Lydia Lawrence, "formerly Beardsall." The "Rank or Profession of Father" was entered as "Coal Miner." The document—Entry No. 297 in the Register of Births No. 77—listed the father's residence as Eastwood (in the Sub-District of Greasley), where the boy was born. The entry did not include the fact that the family residence at that time was on Victoria Street at the southwest corner of Scargill Street —a plain brick house which now has a plaque on its outer wall announcing that this house was the birthplace of D. H. Lawrence.

1887

LAWRENCE FAMILY MOVES FROM VICTORIA STREET TO
THE BREACH

Ada Lawrence Clarke writes: "I remember nothing of
the house where my brother and I were born, for we left
when I was only a few months old and Bert [D. H. Law-
rence] was about two years. The Breach consisted of blocks
of houses belonging to Barber, Walker and Co., the pit-
owners." (ALC, 18) D. H. Lawrence recalled: "It was
a little less common to live in the Breach, which consisted
of six blocks of rather more pretentious dwellings erected
by the company in the valley below" the poorer houses on
the height of Eastwood. (PHX, 134)

1891

LAWRENCE FAMILY MOVES (ABOUT 1891) TO WALKER
STREET, EASTWOOD

"So about five years later we moved again, to Walker
Street"—what was then No. 3. (ALC, 19) Lawrence wrote:
"Go to Walker Street—and stand in front of the third house
—and look across at Crich on the left, Underwood in front
—High Park woods and Annesley on the right: I lived in
that house from 6 to 18, and I know that view better than
any in the world." (AH, 682)

1898

SEPTEMBER 14. LAWRENCE BEGINS DAILY TRIPS TO
NOTTINGHAM

"When I was twelve, I got a county council scholar-
ship, twelve pounds a year, and went to Nottingham High

School." (LL, 364) The entry in the school register shows that Lawrence was No. 733 when he entered the school on September 14, 1898, three days after his thirteenth birthday.

1901

JULY. LEAVES SCHOOL AND PREPARES TO GO TO WORK

Register of Nottingham High School shows that Lawrence "Left July 1901." "After leaving school I was a clerk for three months [for J. H. Haywood, surgical-appliance manufacturer, 9 Castle Gate, Nottingham], then had a very serious pneumonia illness, in my seventeenth year" (LL, 364), apparently in the late autumn or early winter. *Sons and Lovers,* often accurate in matters of small fact, places the beginning of Lawrence's ["Paul Morel's"] illness on December 23. During his "long convalescence" he "spent a month at Skegness [Lincolnshire] with an aunt who kept a 'select' boarding-house on the front." (JC, 28)

1903

LAWRENCE BECOMES PUPIL-TEACHER AT ILKESTON, DERBYSHIRE

After a year as pupil-teacher at the British School in Eastwood, "in 1903 he was drafted, along with other pupil teachers, to the Ilkeston Pupil-Teacher Centre." (JC, 73–74) Confirmed by the Ilkeston Divisional Education Officer in 1949, in a letter to Harry T. Moore. "We . . . attended the pupil-teachers' centre at Ilkeston two or three times a week," (ALC, 44) until 1905, when "for the next year Lawrence taught as an uncertificated teacher at the British School at Eastwood." (JC, 75) It was about 1902 or 1903 that the Lawrence family moved from No. 3 Walker Street to No. 97 Lynn Croft: "A few years after the death of Ernest we went to live in Lynn Croft." (ALC, 42) Lawrence years later remembered living in the house on Walker Street "from the age of 6 to 18." (AH, 682) The departure from Lynn Croft, after Mrs. Lawrence's death in December, 1910 and the break-up of the family, can be definitely dated from a letter of March 8, 1911, in which Lawrence writes his sister, from Croydon: "You are moving tomorrow." (ALC, 69)

1906

SEPTEMBER. LAWRENCE ENTERS NOTTINGHAM UNIVERSITY COLLEGE

"In September, 1906, he entered Nottingham University College as a normal student for a two years' course of training" (JC, 75) and once more made daily trips to Nottingham. His sister Ada is wrong in saying that Lawrence was eighteen when "he went to Nottingham University College." (ALC, 63)

AUGUST. AT MABLETHORPE, LINCOLNSHIRE

"In the August before he entered College the Lawrences made up a party (including myself) and spent a fortnight at Mablethorpe on the Lincolnshire coast." (JC, 126) Lawrence's diary entry for August 9 shows that on that day he "walked to Theddlethorpe." (ALC, 55)

1907

SUMMER. HOLIDAY AT ROBIN HOOD'S BAY, YORKSHIRE

Jessie Chambers, in discussing the 1906 Mablethorpe holiday, speaks of two further "successive occasions when

I spent my annual holiday with the Lawrences and their friends." She mentions that the first of these vacations "was at Robin Hood's Bay"; and the year would be 1907. (JC, 127–128)

1908

SUMMER. HOLIDAY AT FLAMBOROUGH, YORKSHIRE

After discussing the Robin Hood's Bay holiday of 1907, Jessie Chambers says, "And the following year at Flamborough . . ." (JC, 137)

OCTOBER 12. LAWRENCE BEGINS TEACHING AT CROYDON, SURREY (DAVIDSON ROAD SCHOOL)

"From college I went down to Croydon, near London, to teach in a new elementary school." (LL, 364) This was the Davidson Road School, whose Log Book shows that Lawrence began his career there on "October 12, 1908." During his three and a half years at Croydon, Lawrence spent most of his holidays at Eastwood and went there frequently on weekends. Lawrence's residence during his years at Davidson Road School was 12 Colworth Road, Addiscombe, Croydon; he was there as late as September 10, 1911, though by September 25 was at 16 Colworth Road.

1909

Lawrence's first poems are published in the November issue of the *English Review*.

AUGUST. SUMMER HOLIDAY AT SHANKLIN, ISLE OF WIGHT

Jessie Chambers, in discussing 1909, speaks of "August when the Lawrences were on holiday at Shanklin in the Isle of Wight." (JC, 158) George Neville, who was in the party, recalled that "they went up to Cowes in the first week of August to see the review of the fleet for the King and the Czar." (HM, 87)

1910

Lawrence's mother dies in December

AUGUST. SUMMER HOLIDAY ON LANCASHIRE COAST
From George Neville's recollections: "Before Lawrence found his mother ill at Leicester, he had been on a holiday trip in Lancashire, at Blackpool, at Fleetwood, and at Barrow-in-Furness." (HM, 99)

AUGUST 24. AT LEICESTER (20 DULVERTON ROAD)
"Mother is laid-up here, and I must certainly stay with her until Saturday." (AH, 6)

OCTOBER 1. AT BRIGHTON AND NEWHAVEN
Helen Corke remembers: "On the 1st Oct. 1910 he and I walked from Brighton over the cliffs, a 9-mile walk to Newhaven." (HM, 85)

OCTOBER. BACK AT CROYDON (12 COLWORTH ROAD, ADDISCOMBE) FOR FALL TERM
October 18 letter probably written some weeks after his return. (AH, 6)

BY DECEMBER 5. BACK AT EASTWOOD (97 LYNN CROFT)
Letter from there to A. W. McLeod. (HM, 100)

DECEMBER 23. AT CROYDON
Letter from there to A. W. McLeod. (HM, 105)

LATE DECEMBER, 1910. AT BRIGHTON
From recollections of Philip F. T. Smith: "I spent the

Christmas of 1910 at Brighton. Lawrence and his sister visited the town at the same period." (HM, 104)

1911

Lawrence's first book *The White Peacock* is published in January.

BY FEBRUARY 9. AT CROYDON (12 COLWORTH ROAD, ADDISCOMBE)

February 9 letter. Lawrence would have, of course, been in Croydon in January for the reopening of school after Christmas. (ALC, 67)

APRIL 16. AT EASTWOOD FOR EASTER

Letter to his sister Ada, March 27: "It's not long to Easter. I'm glad for the sake of the holiday and of seeing some of my own people." (ALC, 71)

BY APRIL 26. BACK AT CROYDON (12 COLWORTH ROAD, ADDISCOMBE)

(AH, 9)

JULY 31. AT PRESTATYN, NORTH WALES (ROSEWOOD, VICTORIA AVENUE)

"We are installed very happily." (AH, 11)

AUGUST 25. AT QUORN, LEICESTERSHIRE (COLESHAEL, CHEVENEY LANE)

"Until today . . . I have been moving about." (AH, 11)

BY SEPTEMBER 10. BACK AT CROYDON (12 COLWORTH ROAD, ADDISCOMBE, CROYDON)

(AH, 12)

BY SEPTEMBER 25. AT 16 COLWORTH ROAD, ADDIS-
COMBE, CROYDON

Letter indicates changed address for first time. (AH,
12)

? OCTOBER 13–15?. AT THE CEARNE, NEAR EDENBRIDGE,
KENT (EDWARD GARNETT'S COTTAGE)

Letter to Garnett, October 6: "I shall arrive at the
Cearne—this time next week." (AH, 14) Letter to his sister
Ada, apparently written during the week of October 15,
says "I had such a ripping time at Garnett's." (ALC, 77)

BY OCTOBER 20. BACK AT CROYDON (16 COLWORTH
ROAD, ADDISCOMBE)

Letter to Garnett, apparently several days after Lawrence's return. (AH, 14)

1912

On March 9, Lawrence severs his connection with
the Davidson School, Croydon, where he has taught
since October 12, 1908. Early in April, 1912, Lawrence meets Frieda Weekley-Richthofen, wife of
one of his former Nottingham University College
professors, Ernest Weekley. In May, Lawrence and
Mrs. Weekley leave for the Continent. He projects
this experience into some of the poems of *Look! We
Have Come Through!,* published as a collection several years later. In May, his second novel, *The Trespasser,* is published in London. In November, at
Gargnano, Lawrence completes the novel he has
been writing for several years, and changes its name
from *Paul Morel* to *Sons and Lovers.*

JANUARY 1. AT CROYDON, SURREY (16 COLWORTH
ROAD, ADDISCOMBE, CROYDON)

Letters of December 30, 1911 and January 3, 1912 in-

dicate that Lawrence was in Croydon over the turn of the
year, recuperating from an illness. (AH, 18, 20)

ABOUT JANUARY 4–6. "AT RED HILL" (PROBABLY RED-
HILL, SURREY)

"I was away at Red Hill for a couple of days," Lawrence says in a letter of January 7 from Bournemouth. "I
came straight from Red Hill here." (AH, 21) Although there
are several Redhills in England, including one in Nottingham, Lawrence probably stayed en route at Redhill in
Surrey.

JANUARY 6. ARRIVE AT BOURNEMOUTH, HAMPSHIRE
(COMPTON HOUSE, ST. PETER'S ROAD)

"I am actually going to Bournemouth on Saturday"—
the 6th. (AH, 20)

FEBRUARY 3. LEAVE BOURNEMOUTH FOR EDENBRIDGE,
KENT (THE CEARNE, GARNETT'S COTTAGE)

Lawrence on January 29 tells Edward Garnett he will
come to Edenbridge "on the Saturday," or February 3.
(AH, 24)

BY FEBRUARY 10. AT EASTWOOD, NOTTINGHAMSHIRE
(13 QUEEN'S SQUARE)

(AH, 25)

MARCH 6. AT SHIREBROOK, NEAR MANSFIELD, NOTTING-
HAMSHIRE (STATION ROAD PHARMACY)

(AH, 29)

MARCH 8. BACK AT EASTWOOD (QUEEN'S SQUARE)

In late March, Lawrence visited in Staffordshire. (AH,
30, 31)

APRIL 23. AT LEICESTER (20 DULVERTON ROAD, HOME
OF HIS AUNT, MRS. KRENKOW)
   (AH, 36)

APRIL 27–28. AT EDENBRIDGE, KENT
   April 23 letter: Lawrence tells Edward Garnett he
wants "to come to the Cearne on Saturday." April 29 letter
to Garnett indicates that Lawrence has spent the April
27–28 weekend at the Cearne. (AH, 36, 37)

APRIL 29. AT LEICESTER (20 DULVERTON ROAD); TO
EASTWOOD (QUEEN'S SQUARE)
   Letter of this date from Leicester says, "I am going
home today." (AH, 37)

MAY 3. LEAVE LONDON FOR METZ, LORRAINE, GER-
MANY (VIA OSTEND)
   Letter to Frieda (then Mrs. Ernest Weekley) from
Eastwood, May 2: "I shall get in King's Cross tomorrow at
1.25. . . . Eleven pounds will take us to Metz." (FR, 10)
The night journey from Dover across the Channel, to Os-
tend, and the railway trip to Luxembourg and Metz, are
described in the "Continental" chapter of *Women in Love*.

MAY 4. AT METZ (HOTEL DEUTSCHER HOF)
   Date of arrival is apparent from the foregoing. Lawrence in a letter dated May 9, from Trier, says: "I've been
here—since Friday," or since May 3. By "here" he obviously
meant "out of England." (AH, 37)

BY MAY 8. AT TRIER, RHEINPROVINZ, GERMANY (HOTEL
RHEINISCHER HOF)
   (FR, 14)

ABOUT MAY 13. TO WALDBRÖL, RHEINPROVINZ, GER-
MANY ("BEI HERR KARL KRENKOW")

May 9 letter: "I am staying in Trier till next Monday
or Tuesday [13th or 14th]—then, for a week or two, my
address will be . . . Waldbröl, Rheinprovinz." (AH, 37)
Undated letter of second week of May: "I am going up
the Rhine on Monday"—the 13th. (AH, 38) FR records
this all-day journey by means of undated postcards mailed
en route from Niederlahnstein and Hennef. (FR, 18)

MAY 24. TO MUNICH

May 23 letter: "I am going to München tomorrow."
(ALC, 89) June 2 letter: "I came down from the Rhineland
to Munich last Friday week. . . . We stayed in Munich a
night, then went down to Beuerberg for eight days." (AH,
42)

MAY 25–JUNE 1. AT BEUERBERG IM ISARTAL (GAST-
HAUS ZUR POST)

From above and June 2 letter: "We went down to
Beuerberg Saturday week ago." (AH, 44)

JUNE 1. TO ICKING BEI MÜNCHEN, ISARTAL ("BEI PRO-
FESSOR ALFRED WEBER")

June 2 letter: "This is our first morning"—at Icking.
(AH, 44)

AUGUST 5. LEAVE ICKING FOR THE TYROLESE ALPS AND
ITALY

Letter of August 4: "We are going away tomorrow
morning . . . walking to Mayrhofen, about 10 miles from
Innsbruck—stopping there for a week or two . . . then
going on down into Italian Switzerland, where we shall

spend the winter, probably on Lake Garda." (AH, 49) In *Love Among the Haystacks*, the chapter "A Chapel Among the Mountains" describes the couple's spending the first night at "a wayside inn" in the Bavarian Alps.

AUGUST 6. AT A HAY HUT AMONG THE MOUNTAINS

The chapter, "A Hay Hut Among the Mountains," in *Love Among the Haystacks*, describes the second night out from Munich. Also, "We were at the top of the pass and there was a hay-hut in the Alpine meadow. There we slept that night." (AH, 51)

AUGUST 7. TO GLASHÜTTE, BAVARIA (AT "A LITTLE GASTHAUS")

"A Hay Hut Among the Mountains" describes the arrival at Glashütte.

ABOUT MID-AUGUST. AT MAYRHOFEN, TIROL, AUSTRIA ("BEI FRÄULEIN SCHNEEBERGER")

August 19 letter shows Lawrence at Mayrhofen, Zillertal. (AH, 50) Ada Lawrence has an undated postcard, perhaps written earlier, in which Lawrence announces his intention to "stay two or three weeks." (ALC, 89)

ABOUT AUGUST 29. LEAVE MAYRHOFEN FOR STERZING

Undated postcard eight hours before arrival at Sterzing, suggests a three-day trip to that place. (ALC, 87) This accords with David Garnett's reminiscence in *The Golden Echo*.

ABOUT SEPTEMBER 1. AT DOMINICSHÜTTE MIT SCHLEGEISTAL, TIROL, AUSTRIA

Undated postcard, probably September 1, eight hours before arrival at Sterzing, which was apparently reached on September 2. (ALC, 87; AH, 57)

SEPTEMBER 2. AT STERZING AM BRENNER, TIROL, AUS-
TRIA (NOW IN ITALY)

"Last night again we slept in a hut 2000-some odd
hundred meters high"—probably Dominicshütte. (AH, 57)
A postcard wrongly ascribed "1911" is puzzling because it
is plainly written from Sterzing, though it says, "I am
staying here only till tomorrow, Sunday." (ALC, 87) But
the letter of Monday, September 2, to A. W. McLeod, just
quoted, was written on *Monday,* September 2—and Lawrence knew it was Monday. There is a possibility that he
had arrived a day or so earlier, but was spending the nights
in huts in the mountains.

BETWEEN SEPTEMBER 3–6. TO MERAN, BOZEN, AND
TRIENT; TIROL, AUSTRIA

"We set off to walk to Meran [now Merano, Italy],
and got stranded on a wild place . . . and scrambled over
the ridge into the Jaufen house. . . . We got to Bozen [now
Bolzano] . . . Then we moved on to Trient [now Trento]."
(AH, 60)

BY SEPTEMBER 7. AT RIVA, SÜD TIROL, AUSTRIA (VILLA
LEONARDI, VIALE GIOVANNI-PRATI NO. 8)

(AH, 58)

SEPTEMBER 18. MOVE TO GARGNANO, LAGO DI GARDA,
ITALY (VILLA IGEA)

September 23 letter shows Lawrence already at Villa
Igea. (ALC, 91) A somewhat earlier letter, undated, says,
"I am going there on Wednesday." (ALC, 91) This could
not have been on Wednesday the 11th, since a letter of that
date shows him still at Riva. (AH, 60) This evidence indicates that the letters to A. W. McLeod and Edward Garnett (AH, 62, 64), should have been dated, respectively,

September 17—since the letter to McLeod says Lawrence
will move "tomorrow"—and September 16, since the latter
is dated the "Monday" of the week of the move to Gargnano.

Resides at Villa Igea, Gargnano, until March 30, 1913.

1913

Love Poems and Others is published in February
and *Sons and Lovers* in May. Returning to England
during the summer, Lawrence and Mrs. Weekley
meet Edward Marsh, John Middleton Murry, and
Katherine Mansfield. After Lawrence and Mrs.
Weekley cross to the Continent again, Lawrence
resumes work on a novel begun at Gargnano—*The
Sisters,* later to become *The Rainbow* and *Women in
Love.*

MARCH 30. TO SAN GAUDENZIO, GARGNANO

Letter to his sister Ada from Villa Igea, "Tuesday"
[March 25]: "We leave here on Sunday [30th]—go to San
Gaudenzio—which is a farm about 2 miles up the Lake.
Still Gargnano postal district—stay there two or three
days—then go to Verona." (HM, 142) This letter may be
safely dated the 25th. Lawrence on the 11th mentioned a
projected visit to San Gaudenzio "this afternoon" and his
intention of giving up his Villa Igea rooms "at the end of
this month." (AH, 114) In the "Tuesday" letter to his sister
Ada, Lawrence refers to "this holiday," obviously referring
to Easter Week, which began on March 23 that year.

APRIL 11. TO VERONA (HOTEL EUROPA È AQUILA NERA)

April 5 letter: "Frieda must see her sister in Verona
. . . We meet her, I think, next Friday: that is, I believe,
the 11th." (AH, 116)

APRIL 14. LEAVE VERONA FOR MUNICH

April 14 letter: "We are on the move at last—been here a couple of days. . . . We are going tonight to München." (AH, 118)

BY APRIL 17. AT IRSCHENHAUSEN BEI MÜNCHEN (VILLA JAFFE)

(AH, 119)

JUNE 18. LEAVE FOR ENGLAND

June 11 letter: "On this day week we are leaving here for England." (AH, 126) This statement is repeated in an unpublished June 11 postcard to A. W. McLeod.

BY JUNE 21. AT EDENBRIDGE, KENT (THE CEARNE)

(AH, 128)

BY JULY 12. AT KINGSGATE, BROADSTAIRS, KENT (28 PERCY AVENUE)

(AH, 129)

JULY 29–30. LEAVE BROADSTAIRS FOR LONDON

"We are staying till the 29th, then going to London for a day or two." (AH, 131) A letter of the same date to A. W. McLeod says, "We leave here on the 30th—going to the Cearne for a few days." (HM, 152) On July 28, Lawrence wrote Edward Marsh that they would visit him in London "at 1.45 on Wednesday" the 30th. (AH, 132)

ABOUT AUGUST 8. LEAVE ENGLAND FOR GERMANY

"We go back to Bavaria about August 8th." (AH, 132) "We go back to Germany about August 8" (HM, 152)— both letters of July 22.

BY AUGUST 11. AT IRSCHENHAUSEN BEI MÜNCHEN (VILLA JAFFE)

"We are settled down again here now." (AH, 132)

SEPTEMBER 17. LEAVE IRSCHENHAUSEN FOR SWITZERLAND AND ITALY

"Monday" letter to Edward Garnett, which says "We are going away on Wednesday," could only have been written on Monday, September 15 and could only refer to Wednesday the 17th; in the "Monday" letter, Lawrence says, "I'm 28 now"—since September 11. (AH, 141)

SEPTEMBER 18. AT KONSTANZ, BADEN, GERMANY

"I am at present on a steamer in the Lake of Constance going from Überlingen to Constance. . . . I am going to-morrow to Schaffhausen, then walking to Zürich and Lucerne and the Gotthard." (AH, 142)

SEPTEMBER 19. NEAR SCHAFFHAUSEN, SWITZERLAND (INN OF "THE GOLDEN STAG")

The "Italians in Exile" chapter of *Twilight in Italy* describes Lawrence's trip from Constance and through Schaffhausen to a "village of tall, quaint houses flickering its lights on the deep-flowing river." (TWI, 228)

SEPTEMBER 20. TO ZURICH AND DOWN THE LAKE OF ZURICH (TO THE GASTHAUS ZUR POST)

Arrive Zurich. (TWI, 235) "On a steamer down the long lake . . . I landed somewhere on the right bank, about three-quarters of the way down the lake." (TWI, 236) "I found the 'Gasthaus zur Post.'" (TWI, 237)

SEPTEMBER 21. ALONG THE LAKE OF ZURICH

"On I went, by the side of the steamy, reedy lake, walk-

ing the length of it. . . . I went on to a detestable brutal
inn in the town." (TWI, 269, 270)

SEPTEMBER 22. ALONG THE LAKE OF LUCERNE

"I took the steamer down the lake [of Lucerne] to the
very last station. There I found a good German inn." (TWI,
271, 272)

SEPTEMBER 23. AT HOSPENTHAL, CANTON OF URI

"I came, in the early darkness, to the little village with
the broken castle . . . at the point where the track parts,
one way continuing along the ridge to the Furka Pass, the
other swerving over the hill to the left, over the Gotthardt."
(TWI, 286) This is, of course, Hospenthal.

SEPTEMBER 24. TO AIROLO AND BELLINZONA, CANTON
OF TICINO

"So I was content, coming down into Airolo." (TWI,
300) "In the darkness of night, I got into Bellinzona." (TWI,
304)

SEPTEMBER 25. AT LUGANO, CANTON OF TICINO

"In Lugano I stayed at a German hotel." (TWI, 306)

SEPTEMBER 26. AT COMO, ITALY

"I took the steamer down to Como, and slept in a vast
old stone cavern of an inn." (TWI, 310)

SEPTEMBER 27. AT MILAN

"I dared not risk walking to Milan: I took a train. And
there, in Milan, [sat] in the Cathedral Square, on Saturday
afternoon." (TWI, 310)

BY SEPTEMBER 30. AT LERICI, GOLFO DELLA SPEZIA,
ITALY (ALBERGO DELLE PALME)

(AH, 143)

BY OCTOBER 7. AT LERICI, PER FIASCHERINO (VILLINO ETTORE GAMBROSIER)

"We have got a tiny four-roomed cottage . . . down here." (AH, 144)

Resides at Fiascherino until June 8, 1914.

1914

After a London judge declares the Weekley divorce final, Lawrence and Frieda go back to England and are married (at the Kensington Register Office) on July 13. That summer they meet Catherine Carswell and Amy Lowell. Lawrence has been contributing to Edward Marsh's annual volumes of *Georgian Poetry;* now Miss Lowell persuades him to become a contributor also to her quite different annual volumes, *Some Imagist Poets.* In December, Lawrence's first volume of short stories, *The Prussian Officer,* appears.

JUNE 8. LEAVE FIASCHERINO

"We are leaving here on the 8th—next Monday. Frieda goes to Baden for about 10 days." (AH, 199)

JUNE 9. AT TURIN

"In Turin yesterday." (ALC, 93)

JUNE 10. AT AOSTA, SWITZERLAND

"Tonight I sleep in Aosta." (ALC, 92)

JUNE 12. AT HOSPICE DU GRAND ST. BERNARD, SWITZERLAND

"Today we have struggled up here from Aosta." (ALC, 93)

LAST TWO WEEKS OF JUNE(?). ACROSS FRANCE

Lawrence speaks of plans for "walking across Switzerland and France with Lewis, one of the skilled engineers of the Vickers-Maxim works" at Spezia. (AH, 201)

BY JUNE 27. AT LONDON (9 SELWOOD TERRACE, KENSINGTON)

From Sir Edward Marsh's unpublished diary: "Saturday June 27th. Lunched at Moulin d'Or with D. H. and Mrs. Lawrence and Rupert [Brooke], all to Allied Artists at Holland Park." (HM, 163)

JULY 7. AT THE CEARNE, KENT
(AH, 206)

BY JULY 12. BACK IN LONDON (SELWOOD TERRACE)
(AH, 208)

? JULY 18?. AT RIPLEY, DERBYSHIRE

Letter of July 13: "On Saturday I think we are going to Ripley for a few days." (AH, 209)

JULY 31. LEAVE LONDON

"Just getting up to go from London." (AH, 210) Unpublished letter to Mrs. H. G. Wells, July 31: "Today I am going up to the lake district till the 8th."

BY AUGUST 4 OR 5. AT BARROW-IN-FURNESS, LANCASHIRE

"I had been walking in Westmorland. . . . Then we came down to Barrow-in-Furness, and saw that war was declared." (AH, 221)

? BY AUGUST 9?. BACK IN LONDON (SELWOOD TERRACE)

Unpublished letter to Amy Lowell, dated "Sunday"

(apparently August 9): "I am back in London for a week or so. . . . And we are so miserable about the war." Letter to J. B. Pinker, August 10, shows Lawrence back in London. (AH, 211)

BY AUGUST 22. AT CHESHAM, BUCKINGHAMSHIRE (THE TRIANGLE, BELLINGDON LANE)
"Settled in our cottage." (SFD, 247)

Resides at Chesham until January 21, 1915.

ABOUT OCTOBER 27–29. AT LONDON
Letter to Catherine Carswell, October 21: "We should like to come to London one day next week—say Tuesday [27th]—or Thursday [29th]—and stay one night at your house." (AH, 214) Unpublished letter to Mrs. Carswell, October 31: "Thank you so much for having us down."

MID-DECEMBER. VISIT TO DERBYSHIRE
Letter to Amy Lowell, December 18: "We have been in the Midlands seeing my people." (HM, 172)

1915

While living in one of the Meynell family's cottages in Sussex during the early part of the year, the Lawrences meet Bertrand Russell and Lady Ottoline Morrell. In March, Lawrence completes *The Rainbow*, published at the end of September. In the autumn, Lawrence and Murry and Katherine Mansfield plan and publish three issues of a magazine, the *Signature*, for which Lawrence writes his essay, "The Crown" (reprinted ten years later in *Reflections on the Death of a Porcupine*). At this time the

Lawrences meet Aldous Huxley and Dorothy Brett. On November 13, a magistrate orders the suppression of *The Rainbow*.

JANUARY 21. LEAVE CHESHAM

Letter to W. E. Hopkin, January 18: "We leave here Thursday morning [21st]—stay two days in London—go to Pulborough on Saturday." (AH, 219)

? BY JANUARY 23?. AT GREATHAM, PULBOROUGH, SUSSEX

(AH, 219) *See above.*

Resides at Greatham, Pulborough, until July 30.

MARCH 6–7. AT CAMBRIDGE

March 2 letter: "I shall come on Saturday by the train arriving Cambridge 6.2." (RSL, 39)

ABOUT MAY 5–10. IN LONDON

"London next week—Wednesday till Monday." (AH, 230)

ABOUT JUNE 12–16. AT GARSINGTON MANOR, OXFORDSHIRE

"Going to Garsington Saturday–Wednesday." (RSL, 49)

JUNE 21. AT LITTLEHAMPTON, SUSSEX

"The Lawrences came for the day." (CA, 139)

JULY 10–11. IN LONDON

Letter to Ottoline Morrell, July 9: "Going to London for the weekend." (AH, 244) Also, "Monday" [July 12] letter says, "I was in London this weekend." (AH, 245)

JULY 30 TO LITTLEHAMPTON (12 BAYFORD ROAD)

"We are going down to Littlehampton tomorrow to the sea for a few days." (AH, 246)

AUGUST 4. TO LONDON (1 BYRON VILLAS, VALE OF HEALTH, HAMPSTEAD)

"We shall be there on Wednesday [August 4]." (HM, 195)

Resides at 1 Byron Villas until December 21, 1915.

NOVEMBER 8–11. AT GARSINGTON

To Pinker, November 6: "Away from Monday [8th] to Thursday [11th] of next week . . . at Garsington." (AH, 273)

NOVEMBER 29. AT GARSINGTON

To Cynthia Asquith, November 28: "Tomorrow we are going to Garsington for a day or two." (AH, 282)

DECEMBER 3. BACK IN LONDON

Unpublished letter to Catherine Carswell from Garsington, November 29: "We shall be home on Friday [December 3]."

DECEMBER 21. LEAVE 1 BYRON VILLAS, HAMPSTEAD

December 20 letter: "We give up this flat tomorrow." (AH, 301)

DECEMBER 22. AT 2 HURST CLOSE, GARDEN SUBURB, N.W. (LONDON)

"Wednesday [22nd]," postmarked December 23. (AH, 301)

DECEMBER 23. AT RIPLEY, DERBYSHIRE (GROSVENOR ROAD)

Unpublished letter to Ottoline Morrell, December 15: "We are going to my sister's on the 23rd."

DECEMBER 30. ARRIVE AT PADSTOW, CORNWALL (PORTCOTHAN, ST. MERRYN)

"We came here tonight." (AH, 305)

1916

Lawrence completes *Women in Love*. His first travel book, *Twilight in Italy*, comes out in June, and his second collection of poems, *Amores*, in July.

FEBRUARY 29. LEAVE PADSTOW

Letter of "Monday," or February 28: "We leave to-morrow morning." (AH, 338)

FEBRUARY 29. AT ZENNOR, TINNER'S ARMS

(AH, 336, 338)

BY MARCH 22. AT HIGHER TREGERTHEN, ZENNOR

Unpublished letter to Mark Gertler, March 22: "We are getting settled in here." As early as March 8, Lawrence had written J. M. Murry (AH, 341) and Gertler (unpublished) that he had taken a cottage at Higher Tregerthen "and [we] are getting ready to furnish."

Resides at Higher Tregerthen until October 15, 1917.

JUNE 28. TO PENZANCE

"I have to go and join the Colours in Penzance on the 28th." (AH, 356)

BY JUNE 30. BACK AT HIGHER TREGERTHEN

"Complete exemption." (AH, 358)

1917

In October, the military authorities order the Lawrences, as suspected spies, out of Cornwall and tell
them they must avoid living in any "prohibited
area." The *Look! We Have Come Through!* poems
are published in December.

APRIL 14. TO RIPLEY, DERBYSHIRE (VIA BRISTOL)

Unpublished letter to Catherine Carswell, April 11:
"Up to Derbyshire to meet my sisters on Saturday"—the
14th.

APRIL 19. IN LONDON (5 ACACIA ROAD, ST. JOHN'S
WOOD)

Unpublished letter to Catherine Carswell from Grosvenor Road, Ripley, April 16: "I shall come to London on
Thursday"—the 19th.

APRIL 25. TO HERMITAGE, BERKSHIRE (CHAPEL FARM
COTTAGE)

April 28 letter says Lawrence left for Hermitage "on
Wednesday," or April 25. (HM, 231)

APRIL 27. TO CORNWALL

Letter dated "Thursday," which can be only April 26,
says, "Tomorrow I am going back to Cornwall." (AH, 409)
Letter of May 7 from Zennor: "I got back here about ten
days ago." (AH, 411)

JUNE 23. TO BODMIN, CORNWALL

June 26 letter: "I got myself rejected again at Bodmin
on Saturday"—or June 23. (AH, 415)

OCTOBER 15. TO LONDON (32 WELL WALK, HAMP-
STEAD)

October 12 letter: "On Monday [15th] we shall be in
London." (AH, 421)

ABOUT OCTOBER 20. TO 44 MECKLENBURGH SQUARE,
LONDON

Unpublished letter to Cecil Gray, "Friday" October 19:
"Unless we hear tomorrow [about moving into the Grays'
flat], we shall move to 44 Mecklenburgh Square."

ABOUT DECEMBER 14. LEAVE MECKLENBURGH SQUARE
(FOR 13B EARL'S COURT SQUARE)

Letter to Amy Lowell, December 13: "Hilda [Doo-
little] like an angel came to the rescue and lent us her
room. But now she and Richard [Aldington] are come back,
we must yield it up." (SFD, 437)

BY DECEMBER 22. AT HERMITAGE, BERKSHIRE (CHAPEL
FARM COTTAGE)

Unpublished letter to Catherine Carswell, December
22: "We are staying till Thursday—27th—when we come to
London to meet my sister on her way from Portsmouth—
then we shall go with her to the Midlands for a week or
so: after that, probably here again."

DECEMBER 29. AT RIPLEY, DERBYSHIRE (GROSVENOR
ROAD)

"We are staying in the Midlands with my sister for a
few days." (AH, 429)

1918

Lawrence begins magazine publication of some of the *Studies in Classic American Literature*. His volume of *New Poems* comes out in December.

? JANUARY 3, 1918 ?. IN LONDON?

Letter to Gertler, December 29, 1917: "I think we shall be in London next Thursday [January 3, 1918], stay the night perhaps with Kot, then go to the Hermitage." (AH, 429)

BY JANUARY 12. AT HERMITAGE, BERKSHIRE (CHAPEL FARM COTTAGE)

"We are back here from the Midlands—where I just got the wrong kind of chill." (AH, 430)

Resides at Hermitage until May 2.

ABOUT APRIL 5–13. AT RIPLEY, DERBYSHIRE

Letter to Catherine Carswell, "Wednesday" [April 3]: "We are going up to the Midlands Friday." (HM, 241) Letter to Cecil Gray from Hermitage, April 18: "I was up in the Midlands for a week last week." (AH, 442)

MAY 2. TO MIDDLETON-BY-WIRKSWORTH, DERBYSHIRE (MOUNTAIN COTTAGE)

Unpublished letter to J. B. Pinker, April 29: "I am leaving this address on Thursday [May 2] and going to . . . Middleton."

Resides at Middleton-by-Wirksworth until end of April, 1919.

JUNE 14. AT EASTWOOD

Letter to Gertler, June 14: "We are spending a day in the place where I was born—Eastwood." (HM, 242)

AUGUST 12. TO LONDON (5 ACACIA ROAD, ST. JOHN'S WOOD)

Unpublished letter to Enid Hilton, August 8: "We think of coming to London on Monday—12th." Unpublished letter to Enid Hilton, "Wed." [August 14]: "We have been here two days—came Monday."

ABOUT AUGUST 17–20. AT MERSEA ISLAND, ESSEX

Unpublished letter to Catherine Carswell, "Tuesday" [August 20]: "We have just got back from Mersea, where we have spent a weekend."

The letter to J. B. Pinker in the Stanford University collection, a brief business letter dated August 16 from Middleton, may be either a mistake of notation or an attempt to keep correspondence directed to a permanent address.

AUGUST 26. TO UPPER LYDBROOK, FOREST OF DEAN (THE VICARAGE)

Unpublished letter to Enid Hilton, August 24: "On Monday August 26 we are going to 'The Vicarage,' Upper Lydbrook [Ross-on-Wye] Herefordshire."

AUGUST 31. RETURN TO MIDDLETON-BY-WIRKSWORTH

September 1 letter: "We got home quite nicely last evening." (AH, 456)

SEPTEMBER 26. TO DERBY (FOR THE DAY)

September 24 letter: "On Thursday [26th] I've got to go up for medical re-examination." (AH, 459) September

26 letter indicates Lawrence was back at Middleton on same day. (AH, 459)

OCTOBER 7. TO LONDON (32 WELL WALK, HAMPSTEAD)

Unpublished letter to Pinker, October 3: "I shall come to London on Monday"—October 7.

BY OCTOBER 27. TO HERMITAGE, BERKSHIRE (CHAPEL FARM COTTAGE)

Katherine Mansfield's letter to Dorothy Brett, October 27: "Lawrence and Frieda have been in town . . . Now he is gone back to the country." (KM, 191) On November 5, Lawrence wrote Amy Lowell from Hermitage: "We went to London, Frieda and I—got the Flu.—fled here—have recovered—shall probably return soon to Middleton." (SFD, 485)

NOVEMBER 11. IN LONDON

A letter from David Garnett places Lawrence at an Armistice party at Montague Shearman's Adelphi Terrace flat on that evening. (HM, 246) Richard Aldington has said that the Lawrences were at Hermitage that night, like their fictional counterparts in *Kangaroo*, the novel which is unusually accurate in its autobiographical details for the war period. Parts of Garnett's letter not quoted in HM, 246, say: "The discussion between Aldington and myself was continued by letter, and I think I was able to convince him I was right. My memory of the facts was borne out by Mrs. St. John Hutchinson, who was also present." Garnett finally concluded that he and Aldington were both right, and that the Lawrences could have left the party in time to catch the last train for Newbury, which could have returned them to Hermitage before midnight. An unpublished, undated "Monday" letter to Catherine and Donald Carswell, which was probably written on November 11, says: "I am coming to town tomorrow—staying 66, Adelaide Road." But, on hearing that the war had ended, Lawrence could have gone to London late in the day.

NOVEMBER 14 OR 21. RETURN TO MIDDLETON (MOUNTAIN COTTAGE)

In a "Friday" letter to Katherine Mansfield, Lawrence says, "I got home last evening." This section of that letter is unaccountably omitted in AH, 460; a fuller version of it appeared in the *New Adelphi,* June–August, 1930. The "Monday" letter to the Carswells, apparently written on November 11, had said, "Next Monday we shall go back to Middleton." This letter is connected with two earlier un-dated letters by the statement, "Kath Murry told me you fetched the play." Katherine Mansfield told Lady Ottoline Morrell in a November 4 letter (KM, 193), "Lawrence has sent me today a new play of his"—*Touch and Go.* An un-dated, unpublished "Wednesday" letter from Lawrence to Mrs. Carswell says, "This is a mere line to say that I sent the play to Katherine Mansfield, because she is so ill. I wish you would call for it . . . We shall perhaps go back to Middleton next week—shall be a night or two in town." This letter may safely be dated November 6 because the "Satur-day" letter (also published) which closely follows ("Just a line to say, did you get the play from Katherine Murry—") was written on November 9: it mentions the false Armistice report of November 7: "We had a marvelous Peace report on Thursday night—great celebrations and hurrahing. We still feel a little crestfallen." Since both the November 6 and 11 letters mention an early return to Middleton, and since Lawrence arrived there on a Thursday, the probable dates are November 14 or 21. In the undated "Friday" letter, previously mentioned, to Katherine Mansfield, he said, "To-morrow I am going to Ripley and Eastwood, for the week-end" of either November 16–17 or 23–24.

DECEMBER 19. AT MATLOCK, DERBYSHIRE

December 20 letter: "We went to Matlock yesterday." (AH, 465)

DECEMBER 25. AT RIPLEY (GROSVENOR ROAD)

"We got your parcel on Christmas morning. We had started off . . . when the postman loomed round the cor-ner." (AH, 467) Earlier: "We are going across to my sister's on Christmas day." (AH, 466)

DECEMBER 27. RETURN TO MIDDLETON

"Tonight we are going back to Middleton." (AH, 468)

1919

In November, the month which marks the publica-tion of *Bay: A Book of Poems,* Lawrence leaves Eng-land, never to return again except for three short visits. In Florence in November, 1919, Norman Douglas introduces him to Maurice Magnus, of whom Lawrence is later to write a controversial bio-graphical sketch.

? MID-FEBRUARY ?. TO RIPLEY (GROSVENOR ROAD)

During the world-wide epidemic of influenza in 1919, Lawrence became seriously ill, and spent some time at Ripley. Richard Aldington has suggested "that Frieda grew alarmed and took him to his sister's home where he was warmer and more comfortable and could be better nursed." (RA, 242) Because of the severity of this illness, Lawrence probably wrote no letters during this period, which makes exact dating difficult. He was at Middleton on February 9, reporting that he had "had a cold and been in bed," but was nevertheless now going for walks in the snow. (AH, 472) It was perhaps soon after this that he went to Ripley. On March 2, he wrote Harriet Monroe: "I have been struggling with the 'flu for a month and am still in bed." (AH, 478) This was of course written from Ripley, although it carries a Mountain Cottage, Middleton, heading; but the letter was going overseas, and Lawrence was merely indicating his permanent address.

ABOUT MARCH 16. RETURN TO MIDDLETON (MOUNTAIN COTTAGE)

The date of Lawrence's return to Middleton is suggested by internal evidence in published letters. One of them (AH, 474), tells Murry: "Today I am going to make an effort to creep downstairs." Dated only "Thursday," the letter must have been written on March 6, for in a letter of March 7, Katherine Mansfield definitely refers to it in a note to Murry (MTM, 312), as having "just come." In a "Tuesday" letter to Mrs. Carswell, Lawrence reports: "I am getting well—but am so weak. I go downstairs to tea." (AH, 475) This would probably be five days after the letter to Murry, or Tuesday, March 11. Lawrence further tells Mrs. Carswell, "On Sunday I am to be taken back to Mountain Cottage—only 20 minutes in a motor-car." Presumably, then, he went back about Sunday, March 16. He writes Gertler from Middleton—where he says he is "an irritable sort of convalescent"—on March 20. (AH, 478)

ABOUT MAY 1. TO HERMITAGE, BERKSHIRE (CHAPEL FARM COTTAGE)

Letter to Amy Lowell, April 5: "We are going down there at the end of the month." (SFD, 493) Unpublished letter to Catherine Carswell from Shirley House, Ripley, Derbyshire, dated only "Tuesday" [probably April 29]: "We are going down to Hermitage on Thursday or Friday—this week anyhow—for good—giving up Mountain Cottage." Unpublished letter to J. B. Pinker, from Hermitage, May 5, thanks him "for the cheque for fifty-five pounds which came so nicely on Saturday"—or May 3—indicating that the Lawrences had just moved in.

Resides at Hermitage until July 28.

JULY 3. TO LONDON

July 3 letter to Amy Lowell: "I am going to London today to see about things—a passport for Frieda, etc."—a passport to Germany. (SFD, 499)

JULY 8. BACK TO HERMITAGE

Unpublished letter to Helen Thomas [Mrs. Edward Thomas], from Hermitage, July 9: "I got back here last evening—no nearer to America." Lawrence also wrote to Eleanor Farjeon on July 9: "I was in town a day or two." (AH, 485) The evidence thus suggests that he went to London on Thursday, July 3, then for the weekend to Mrs. Thomas's [The Forge House, Oxford, Kent], and back to London for Monday and Tuesday July 7 and 8, returning to Hermitage on the latter date after meeting with delays in attempting to get his passport for America.

JULY 28. TO PANGBOURNE, BERKSHIRE (MYRTLE COTTAGE)

Letter to Catherine Carswell, "Friday" [possibly August

15], from Pangbourne: "We are here—since July 28." (HM, 253)

AUGUST 25. BACK TO HERMITAGE, BERKSHIRE (CHAPEL FARM COTTAGE)

Letter to Mrs. Carswell from Pangbourne, "Friday": "We are here, I think, till the 25th—then to Hermitage, either to stay in the [Chapel Farm] Cottage or with those farm girls"—at Grimsbury Farm, Long Lane, near Newbury, Berkshire. (HM, 253) An unpublished "Wednesday" letter to Mrs. Carswell from Pangbourne [probably Wednesday, August 20]: "We are here till Monday [25th]—then to Hermitage."

BY SEPTEMBER 2. AT GRIMSBURY FARM, NEAR NEWBURY, BERKSHIRE

"We are here for the time." (AH, 488)

BY SEPTEMBER 15. BACK AT HERMITAGE

An unpublished letter of this date to G. G. Macfarlane, Catherine Carswell's brother, shows that Lawrence was now back at Chapel Farm Cottage.

? NOVEMBER 10 ?. TO LONDON (5 ACACIA ROAD, ST. JOHN'S WOOD)

Letter to Catherine Carswell, "Thursday," probably written on November 6: "I am preparing to go to Italy." (AH, 489) "I shall come to London on Monday, most probably"—or November 10. This letter also says, "I went to the Midlands last week . . . I've been stuck indoors with a cold this week." (AH, 490)

NOVEMBER 14. LEAVE ENGLAND FOR ITALY

Unpublished letter to Mrs. Rosalind Baynes (now Mrs. A. E. Popham), from London, dated only "Wednesday," which was written on Wednesday, November 12: "I am going by train on Friday morning . . . I leave Charing Cross at 8.0 a.m." Another unpublished letter to Rosalind Popham, headed "Train" and dated November 17: "I got to Paris about 6.30 p.m. Friday evening . . . left Gare de Lyon 9.30 p.m."

NOVEMBER 15–17. NEAR TURIN, ITALY (SIR WALTER BECKER'S VILLA, VAL SALICE)

Unpublished "Train" letter of November 17 to Rosalind Popham, after describing departure from Paris on the night of Friday the 14th, says: "Arrive"[d] Modane (frontier) about 1.30 p.m. next day—Turin 8.0 p.m. (Saturday). . . . I left Turin this morning at 8.30—am now sitting in a motionless train, beside a lovely sunset sea, and it is 5.30. From Genoa for 50 miles it is all sea. . . . I shall stop the night in Spezia, go to Florence in the morning."

NOVEMBER 18–19. AT LERICI (ALBERGO DELLE PALME, LERICI, GOLFO DELLA SPEZIA)

Letter from Lerici to Lady Cynthia Asquith is misdated in the text as November 8; Lawrence was there on the *18th*. "I couldn't get any farther than this yesterday." (AH, 490; 491)

NOVEMBER 19. TO FLORENCE (PENSIONE BALESTRI, 5 PIAZZA MENTANA)

Letter from Lerici, which should be dated November 18: "I am going to Florence tomorrow." (AH, 491)

DECEMBER 9. TO ROME (AT ELLESINA SANTORO'S— CATHERINE CARSWELL'S COUSIN)

Unpublished letter to Rosalind Popham, from Florence, November 28: "We stay here till about Dec. 9th—then to Rome for 5 or 6 days: and then to Picinisco." A "Sat. evening,

Nov. 29" letter (incorrectly assigned to 1918 rather than 1919), says definitely, "We shall stay here till Dec. 9th—then to Rome." (ALC, 95)

BY DECEMBER 16. AT PICINISCO (PROVÍNCIA DI CA-SERTA, PRESSO ORAZIO CERVI)
(AH, 491)

DECEMBER 22. LEAVE PICINISCO
"On Monday (22nd) we did extricate ourselves. . . . We got to Naples, caught the Capri boat at 3.0 p.m." (AH, 495)

DECEMBER 23. ARRIVE AT CAPRI (PALAZZA FERRARO)
(AH, 495)

Resides at Palazza Ferraro until February 26, 1920.

1920

In June, Lawrence completes the revisions of *Studies in Classic American Literature* (slightly revised again later, in America). November sees the publication of two novels: *Women in Love,* in a limited edition "for subscribers only," in New York—and *The Lost Girl,* in London. The latter wins (in 1921) the James Tait Black prize from Edinburgh University; a hundred pounds.

JANUARY 27. AT AMALFI, ITALY
Postcard of January 27: "We have come on a trip to the mainland tired of post strike and railway strike and no letters and no work possible." (ALC, 146) (Postcard incorrectly assigned to 1929 in ALC)

BY FEBRUARY 1. BACK TO CAPRI (PALAZZA FERRARO)

Letter to Mrs. Carswell, February 5: "I had your letter at last—after all these strikes. . . . We went a little excursion on the mainland last week [week ended on January 31], down the Amalfi coast." (AH, 505, 506)

FEBRUARY 19. TO ABBEY OF MONTECASSINO, PROVÍNCIA FROSINONE, ITALY

Lawrence diary note for February 21: "Returned from Montecassino." He had apparently been away from Capri three days, though his references to the visit, in his Introduction to Maurice Magnus's *Memoirs of the Foreign Legion,* are somewhat confusing. When he wrote of the experience two years later, Lawrence's visual memory remained sharp, but his chronology had become hazy; he twice (Introduction, pp. 19, 24) wrote of the visit as having occurred in January, and his jumping from evening to afternoon sequences adds to the difficulties. But he mentions only three mornings: when he left Capri for the mainland on the day of his arrival at Montecassino, the first morning at the monastery, and the morning—apparently the following one —of his departure (pp. 20, 28 and 39, respectively). The evidence suggests that Lawrence went to Montecassino on the 19th and left on the 21st.

An inquiry to Montecassino, as to when Lawrence might have registered there, brought a reply ("23 maggio 1953") that was a melancholy echo of World War II: "Non conserviamo il registro delle firme dei visitatori del 1920: esso è andato distrutto insieme a gran parte della nostra biblioteca privata."

FEBRUARY 21. BACK TO CAPRI (PALAZZA FERRARO)

"Returned from Montecassino." (LDN, 89)

FEBRUARY 26. TO SICILY

"Tomorrow [26th] I am going by sea to Sicily—from Naples. If I find a house we shall go over." (ALC, 96) Mrs. Francis Brett Young, in a letter of October 26, 1953 to Harry T. Moore, reports that she and her husband were on this "journey with Lawrence, when we went from place to place with him to find a house, which was finally the one at Taormina"—after Syracuse and Girgenti.

BY MARCH 4. AT TAORMINA, SICILY (FONTANA VEC-CHIA)

"I have found such a charming house here in a big garden." (ALC, 96)

Resides at Fontana Vecchia, Taormina, until February 20, 1922.

APRIL 25. IN SYRACUSE, SICILY

"Friends invited us down to Syracuse for a few days." (ALC, 97) (Postcard of April 25, wrongly attributed to 1921 in ALC.) Also to Bronte, Mianiace; letter to Lady Cynthia Asquith from Taormina, May 7: "Bronte is just under Etna —and this Mr. Nelson-Hood has a place there—his ducal estate. We went to see him." (AH, 511)

MAY 16. TO VALETTA, MALTA (GREAT BRITAIN HOTEL; LATER, OSBORNE HOTEL)

Letter to Martin Secker from Valetta, May 24: "We came here for two days—kept here for eight by the Sicilian steamer strike." (AH, 513)

MAY 28. RETURN TO TAORMINA (FONTANA VECCHIA)

Letter to Mrs. Carswell: "We only got back tonight, after some 11 days." (HM, 271)

AUGUST 2. LEAVE FOR ITALY

"Leave for Anticoli"—now Fiuggi, Província di Roma. (LDN, 91)

AUGUST 12. LEAVE ANTICOLI

Unpublished letter to Rosalind Popham, August 10: "We move north on Thursday [12th]—get to Milan about 17th."

BY SEPTEMBER 10. AT FLORENCE (VILLA CANOVAIA, SAN GERVASIO)

Unpublished letter to J. B. Pinker from Florence on that date thanks him for a cheque "which I received yesterday." Letter to Amy Lowell, September 12: "Frieda wanted to go to Germany: so I have been wandering around Lake Como and Venice, and now am here for a while in an explosion-shattered, rambling old villa." (HM, 273) Unpublished letter to Pinker, September 16: "Am in Florence till the beginning of October."

OCTOBER 3. IN VENICE (PONTE DELLE MERAVIGIE 1061)

Unpublished postcard to Amy Lowell, October 3: "Am back here waiting for Frieda, who comes in a day or two."

OCTOBER 14. TO FLORENCE

October 13 letter from Venice: "We are going to Florence tomorrow—shall be in Taormina next week." (EM, 233) They also probably visited Rome again: an unpublished letter to Hilda Brown, now Mrs. Cotterell, from Venice, October 12: "We are leaving on Sunday for Rome."

OCTOBER 20. ARRIVE BACK AT TAORMINA (FONTANA VECCHIA)

"Returned to Taormina." (LDN, 91)

1921

In March, Oxford University Press publishes Lawrence's school text, *Movements in European History*, with Lawrence taking the pseudonym, "Lawrence H. Davison." Two more of his books receive first publication in New York: *Psychoanalysis and the Unconscious* in March, and *Sea and Sardinia* in December. Lawrence completes most of the *Birds, Beasts and Flowers* collection of poems (except for the few added later in New Mexico), and he finishes his novel *Aaron's Rod*.

JANUARY 4. LEAVE FOR SARDINIAN JOURNEY

"Going to Palermo for Sardinia (?) in the morning." (LDN, 92) Arrival at 6:30 P.M. (SRD, 25)

JANUARY 5. ABOARD *City of Trieste*

At Levanzo by evening. (SRD, 45)

JANUARY 6. ARRIVE AT CAGLIARI, SARDINIA

City of Trieste into port in afternoon. (SRD, 61)

JANUARY 7. TO MANDAS, BY BUS

(SRD, 87)

JANUARY 8. TO SORGONO, BY TRAIN

(SRD, 105)

JANUARY 9. TO NUORO, BY TRAIN

(SRD, 148)

62									[1921]

JANUARY 10. TO TERRANOVA, BY BUS; STEAMER FOR
MAINLAND
Departure by steamer. (SRD, 180; 187)

JANUARY 11. ARRIVE AT CIVITAVÉCCHIA, PROVÍNCIA DI
ROMA, ITALY
Arrival at Rome. Arrival at Naples (night). Departure,
aboard *City of Trieste,* for Sicily. (SRD, 189; 191; 197)

JANUARY 12. ARRIVE PALERMO, SICILY
(SRD, 207)

JANUARY 13. RETURN TO TAORMINA (FONTANA VEC-
CHIA)
January 14 entry: "Came back from Sardinia last night."
(LDN, 92)

MARCH 11. TO PALERMO
"Leave for Palermo—Frieda en route for Baden-
Baden." (LDN, 92)

MARCH 14. BACK TO TAORMINA.
March 15 entry: "Returned last night from Palermo."
(LDN, 92)

APRIL 9. TO PALERMO, CAPRI, AND MAINLAND
Three April 4 letters announce departure. (AH, 519,
520, 521) The last of these says: "I am leaving Taormina on
Saturday—Palermo—Rome—then perhaps a walking tour
in Sardinia [on which he did not go]: then I don't know: to
Germany probably." (AH, 521)

ABOUT APRIL 19. LEAVE CAPRI
April 18 postcard (incorrectly assigned to 1919): "Am
staying here with friends for a few days—leave for Rome

tomorrow or Wednesday [20th]—then direct to Baden."
(ALC, 95)

APRIL 22. AT FLORENCE

"I had your letter in Rome. . . . I am going direct to
Baden-Baden now." (AH, 521, 522)

APRIL 23. LEAVE FLORENCE

Unpublished postcard to Catherine Carswell, postmarked "Florence 22 IV 21": "Tomorrow I leave here for
Switzerland and Germany."

ABOUT APRIL 26. AT BADEN-BADEN (LUDWIG-
WILHELMSTIFT; THEN HOTEL KRONE, EBERSTEINBURG)

May 17 letter: "Have been here now three weeks."
(AH, 523) Another letter shows Lawrence at Baden-Baden
as early as April 28. (AH, 522)

JULY 16. AT KONSTANZ, BADEN (GERMANY)

Unpublished letter to Catherine Carswell, July 16: "We
are on our way to the Austrian Tyrol—hope to cross this
lake Monday [18th]."

ABOUT JULY 19. ARRIVE AT THUMERSBACH ZELL-AM-
SEE, AUSTRIA (VILLA ALPENSEE)

From above. Letter from Zell incorrectly dated *July* 7.
(AH, 526)

LATE AUGUST. LEAVE THUMERSBACH, ZELL-AM-SEE,
FOR FLORENCE

Unpublished postcard to Catherine Carswell, dated
August 15 by Lawrence but not postmarked at Zell until
August 21, says: "We are leaving here at the end of the
week—shall be in Florence early next week." An unpublished card to Amy Lowell, postmarked at Zell either Au-

gust 21, Sunday, or August 27, Saturday, says: "We are leaving this week for Florence."

BY AUGUST 29. AT FLORENCE (32 VIA DEI BARDI)

A September 1 letter from Florence mentions the arrival of a friend "two days ago," implying that the Lawrences had arrived before then. (AH, 530)

SEPTEMBER 21. LEAVE FLORENCE FOR CAPRI

Unpublished postcard to Mrs. Carswell, written during a brief visit to Siena and dated only "Wednesday" [21st], postmarked Florence on the 22nd, says: "We must leave tonight [presumably the 21st]—must get to Capri."

ABOUT SEPTEMBER 22–27. AT CAPRI

Earl Brewster recalled, "Lawrence and his wife visited us for several days on their return journey to Taormina." (BR, 26) Lawrence in a letter after his return to Taormina, wrote: "I am so glad we came to Capri." (BR, 28)

SEPTEMBER 27 OR 28. RETURN TO TAORMINA (FONTANA VECCHIA)

Letter to Catherine Carswell, September 29: "We got home last night in a whirlwind and rain." (AH, 530) But a letter to Brewster which says, "Got here in the dark and rain of last night," is dated "Wednesday"—or September 28. (BR, 27) Lawrence's subsequent recollection of the time is mistaken; the diary entry for October 26 is: "Got back a month ago, September 23." (LDN, 93)

1922

Aaron's Rod is published in New York in April, with
Fantasia of the Unconscious and the *England, My
England* stories following in October. During the
summer months he spends in Australia, Lawrence
writes his novel *Kangaroo.*

FEBRUARY 20. LEAVE TAORMINA FOR NAPLES, EN
ROUTE TO CEYLON

Diary entry for Saturday, February 18: "Packing for
Ceylon—leave Monday." (LDN, 95) "Sunday" letter, obviously February 19, says, "Tomorrow at 10.34 we leave here:
eat at Messina, where we must change, arrive at 8.30 at
Palermo, then to the Hotel Panoramus. . . . Thursday to
Naples by boat, there at the Hotel Santa Lucia. Then on
the S.S. *Osterley,* Orient Line, to Ceylon." (FR, 106)

FEBRUARY 20–23. AT PALERMO (HOTEL PANORAMUS)
See above.

FEBRUARY 23. TO NAPLES (HOTEL SANTA LUCIA, QUAI
PARTENOPE)
See February 20.

FEBRUARY 26. DEPART AT 8 P.M., ABOARD S.S. *Osterley,*
FOR CEYLON

Unpublished postcard to Catherine Carswell, from
Naples, dated "Saturday" and postmarked on that day, the
25th: "We leave tomorrow on the *Osterley.*"

MARCH 2. AT PORT SAID

"We arrive on Thursday at Port Said." (FR, 107)

ABOUT MARCH 13. ARRIVE AT COLOMBO, CEYLON

"We . . . expect to come to Colombo on Monday"—the 13th. (AH, 546)

BY MARCH 23. AT "ARDNAREE," LAKE VIEW ESTATE, KANDY (CEYLON)

March 25 letter: "The Prince of Wales was here [at Kandy] on Thursday"—the 23rd (AH, 547)

APRIL 24. LEAVE CEYLON ABOARD R.M.S. *Orsova*

April 22 letter: "We sail for West Australia on Monday" —24th. (AH, 550)

MAY 4. ARRIVE AT FREMANTLE, WEST AUSTRALIA

Lawrence's postcard from Kandy to Mrs. A. L. Jenkins says: "Shall come right on—probably by the boat from Colombo, arriving Fremantle May 4." (Quoted in H. E. L. Priday's "D. H. Lawrence in Australia—Some Unpublished Correspondence," *Southerly,* Number One, 1954, p. 4.) A letter or card from Lawrence to Mrs. Luhan announces his arrival in Australia on *April* 4. (ML, 21) This is the kind of misdating that sometimes occurs in his letters written early in a new month.

ABOUT MAY 7. DARLINGTON, WEST AUSTRALIA

Addition to Mrs. Luhan's letter or card quoted above, dated "Sunday"—probably May 7—says, "Came out into the bush." (ML, 21) Mrs. A. L. Jenkins "showed the Lawrences around Perth, fixed them up temporarily in a guest house at Darlington." (Priday, *Southerly,* Number One, p. 4)

MAY 18. LEAVE FREMANTLE FOR SYDNEY (ABOARD s.s. *Malwa*)

"Thursday [18th] we go by the P. & O. boat *Malwa* to

Adelaide, Melbourne, and Sydney. We stay at Adelaide a day, sleep a night at Melbourne, and arrive at Sydney on the 27th." (FR, 122)

MAY 27. ARRIVE AT SYDNEY

"We got to Sydney on Saturday"—the 27th. (FR, 124) This letter, dated May 28, should be dated the 29th; Lawrence had his dates about this period confused. Diary entry for July 3: "Landed in Sydney on Saturday May 26th"—a calendar impossibility. (LDN, 96)

MAY 29. TO THIRROUL, NEW SOUTH WALES ("WYE-WORK")

"Came here on the Monday"—or the 29th—after landing at Sydney. (LDN, 96) Letters dated from Thirroul on May 28 (AH, 553; FR, 124) are probably wrong; Lawrence apparently had the days of the week correct, but not the calendar dates.

AUGUST 10. LEAVE AUSTRALIA, FROM SYDNEY, FOR SAN FRANCISCO (ABOARD THE *Tahiti*)

"We think of sailing on 10th August via Wellington and Tahiti to San Francisco—land on 4th September. Then go to Taos." (AH, 556)

AUGUST 15. AT WELLINGTON, NEW ZEALAND

(ALC, 99) Also, an unpublished postcard to Mrs. Carswell: "Here for a day."

AUGUST 20. AT AVATIU, RARATONGA

(ALC, 99; BR, 60.)

AUGUST 22. AT PAPEETE, TAHITI

(ALC, 99) Also, an unpublished card to Mrs. Carswell: "Here till tomorrow afternoon."

SEPTEMBER 4. ARRIVE AT SAN FRANCISCO (PALACE HOTEL)

"We arrived yesterday." (FR, 154)

SEPTEMBER 8. LEAVE SAN FRANCISCO FOR LAMY AND SANTE FE, NEW MEXICO

September 8 letter: "We leave tonight for Santa Fe." (SFD, 621)

SEPTEMBER 10. ARRIVE AT LAMY; OVERNIGHT AT SANTA FE

This is the only possible date for the overnight stay at Bynner's house described in ML, 40–41, and in BYN, 1–8. *See date below.*

SEPTEMBER 11. ARRIVE AT TAOS (MRS. LUHAN'S HOUSE)

Postcard from Taos, September 12: "We got here yesterday." (BR, 60)

SEPTEMBER 14–19. AT JICARILLA APACHE RESERVATION, RIO ARRIBA AND SANDOVAL COUNTIES

Letter to Curtis Brown, September 20: "I was away five days motoring to the Apache country to an Indian Feast there, so only got your letter last night"—upon returning to Taos. (HM, 300)

DECEMBER 1. TO DEL MONTE RANCH, LOBO, NEW MEXICO

November 30 note to Antonio Luhan was written, on point of departure, on a Thursday; "Saturday" note to Mabel Luhan, "Got here after a struggle yesterday," was obviously written on December 2. (ML, 106)

Resides at Del Monte Ranch until March 18, 1923.

1923

Three short novels by Lawrence appear in London in March as *The Ladybird* and in New York in April as *The Captain's Doll*. During his two months' stay at Chapala, Jalisco, Mexico, Lawrence works on his novel, *The Plumed Serpent*. By August he is in New York for first publication of *Studies in Classic American Literature*. The following month, *Kangaroo* comes out in London and, in September, *Birds, Beasts and Flowers* makes its first appearance in New York. In the autumn, while traveling in Mexico, Lawrence rewrites *The House of Ellis*, a novel sent to him in manuscript by an Australian friend, Mollie Skinner; Lawrence rechristens the story *The Boy in the Bush*.

MARCH 18. LEAVE DEL MONTE RANCH

Letter to Bynner, in Santa Fe, March 8: "I am fixing definitely to leave here on the 18th, and arrive in Santa Fe either on the 20th or 21st." (BYN, 17)

MARCH 19. LEAVE TAOS FOR SANTA FE

"I expect to catch the stage on Monday morning"—the 19th. (BYN, 17)

? MARCH 20?. LEAVE SANTA FE FOR LAMY AND EL PASO

Bynner remembers the Lawrences' staying "overnight" in Santa Fe and, the next day, seeing "them off at the Santa Fe station for Lamy, Albuquerque, El Paso, and Mexico." (BYN, 18) It is possible, however, that Lawrence left Santa Fe on the 21st; a note of the 14th to Bynner suggests either a "Tuesday night" or a Wednesday departure.

MARCH 21. LEAVE EL PASO FOR MEXICO CITY, "IN AN UNKEMPT PULLMAN"

March 21 postcard from El Paso: "We cross the frontier into Mexico this morning." (PHX, 104 and ALC, 101)

MARCH 23. ARRIVE AT MEXICO CITY (HOTEL REGIS; LATER, HOTEL MONTE CARLO, AVENIDA URUGUAY)

Postcard of "Saturday" [24th]: "Arrived wearily last night—went to a big American hotel—didn't like it at all—found this little Italian hotel." (MER, 264) During their stay in Mexico City, the Lawrences—with Witter Bynner and Willard Johnson—made various trips to near-by places. As Lawrence reported in a postcard of April 11 to Bessie Freeman, "We motored out to the pyramids"—at Teotihuacán. (HM, 311) Bynner recalls "occasional short trips to such places at Xochimilco and its canals," and to "the ruined monastery, El Desierto de los Leónes." (BYN, 23) Lawrence, in the card to Mrs. Freeman, April 11: "We also stayed at Cuernavaca . . . And tomorrow we set off for Puebla, Tehuacán, Orizaba."

APRIL 11. LEAVE MEXICO CITY FOR PUEBLA AND ORIZABA

APRIL 21. RETURN TO MEXICO CITY (HOTEL MONTE CARLO)

"I found your letter here," indicating recent arrival. (MER, 292) The same applies to a letter to Amy Lowell, April 21. (SFD, 638) Several letters or cards from Orizaba also on that date to Mrs. Carswell, unpublished; also ALC, 106, MER, 274; the last says: "We go back to Mexico City tomorrow, and I shall find mail." Probably Lawrence on the 20th thought he was writing on the 21st. A description of the trip to Puebla and other towns (including Cholula and Atlixco) is in BYN, 35–43.

APRIL 27. TO GUADALAJARA AND CHAPALA

"Friday" [April 27] letter from Frieda Lawrence: "To-night Lawrence goes to Guadalajara." (MER, 293) Lawrence's letter (FR, 160), "Tomorrow I go to Guadalajara," is dated the 27th but was possibly written on the 26th. (FR, 160)

MAY 2. AT CHAPALA, JALISCO (CALLE ZARAGOZA 4)

Diary entry May 3: "Came in this house yesterday." (LDN, 98)

Resides at Calle Zaragoza 4, Chapala, until July (9?).

JUNE 26–27. AT OCOTLAN AND TIRZAPAN

Diary entry June 27: "Came back from trip to Ocotlán [misspelled *Ocottan* in the book] and Tizapán." (LDN, 98) The "Today is Sunday" letter from Frieda Lawrence to Merrild, misdated by him as June 17, was written on June 24; Lawrence takes over the letter with the statement: "We are going up on Tuesday [26th] up to Ocotlán on the lake." (MER, 303) Lawrence's "Wednesday" letter, postmarked from Chapala, June 27, says: "We were away two days traveling on the lake." (AH, 575)

ABOUT JULY 5–7. BOAT TRIP ON LAKE CHAPALA TO TUXCUECA

Bynner describes the trip, sailing "in what they call a canoa"; trip ended by storms and illness; the Lawrences went to Guadalajara and are among those described as returning "to Chapala, three or four days later." (BYN, 167–172)

ABOUT JULY 9–10. LEAVE CHAPALA FOR MEXICO CITY AND NEW YORK

Letter of Tuesday, July 2: "We are going up to New York next week." (AH, 577) In a June 7 letter, Lawrence had spoken of his intention to "go to Mexico City and sail from Vera Cruz for New York." (CC, 176) This led Richard Aldington to state that the Lawrences had followed this route, but in "a postcard from somewhere in Texas," Lawrence described a train journey: "It rained all the way in Mexico." (BYN, 187)

BY JULY 15. AT NEW ORLEANS (HOTEL DE SOTO)

"Sunday" letter postmarked July 15 [Sunday that year]: "Here we are—got so far on the journey to New York." (AH, 577)

JULY 17. LEAVE NEW ORLEANS FOR NEW YORK

"Tuesday" letter [July 17th]: "We go today to Washington, for New York." (RMM, 177)

JULY 19. ARRIVE AT NEW YORK

Unpublished letter of "Friday" July 20 from New York: "We got in yesterday—Today are going out to New Jersey to stay in a cottage."

JULY 20–AUGUST 20. AT UNION HILL, DOVER, NEW JERSEY ("MR. HAMMERSLAUGH'S COTTAGE")

Date of arrival evident from foregoing. There were occasional trips to New York City, until Frieda Lawrence's departure for England on August 18. On that day, Lawrence writes Amy Lowell: "I am leaving this cottage for good on

Monday [20th]—expect to leave New York on Tuesday."
(SFD, 639)

AUGUST 22. AT BUFFALO

August 22 letter from Buffalo: "I have got so far—I am
staying in Buffalo till Friday [24th] at Mrs. Freeman's.
Shall probably stay a day in Chicago, also—perhaps—in
Salt Lake City." (MER, 311)

AUGUST 25. LEAVE BUFFALO FOR CHICAGO

Lawrence on August 28 writes to thank Mrs. Freeman
"for the four full days in Buffalo." (HM, 320)

AUGUST 26. IN CHICAGO

November 20 letter to Harriet Monroe: "In September
I was in Chicago for a day"; it was of course really at the
end of August. (AH, 594) The "Tuesday" letter to Mrs.
Freeman, written aboard the Los Angeles Limited on
August 28, says: "It rained and fogged in Chicago." (HM,
320)

AUGUST 30. ARRIVE AT LOS ANGELES (UNION PACIFIC)
(MER, 312)

AUGUST 31. TO SANTA MONICA (HOTEL MIRAMAR)
(MER, 312)

SEPTEMBER 9. TO SANTA BARBARA
(MER, 315)

SEPTEMBER 10. TO LOMPOC
(MER, 316)

BY SEPTEMBER 12. BACK IN LOS ANGELES (628 WEST 27TH STREET)

September 12 letter from Los Angeles. (AH, 584)

SEPTEMBER 25. LEAVE LOS ANGELES FOR MEXICO (SOUTHERN PACIFIC RAILROAD)

September 24 letter: "I am setting off tomorrow with a Danish friend, down the west coast of Mexico." (AH, 585)

? SEPTEMBER 26?. AT PALM SPRINGS (HOTEL LA PALMA)

Unpublished letter to Mrs. Bessie Freeman from Palm Springs indicates brief stopover there on "Wednesday September 25," an impossible date; Wednesday was the 26th. Lawrence's postcard to Knud Merrild from Palm Springs also says "Wednesday." (MER, 330) He may have arrived on the 25th and stayed overnight at the La Palma, leaving for Mexico early on the 26th.

SEPTEMBER 27. ARRIVE AT GUAYMAS, SONORA, MEXICO

Letter to Merrild from Lawrence's traveling companion, K. G. Gótzsche: "We arrived this morning at Guaymas." (MER, 332)

ABOUT OCTOBER 1. LEAVE FOR NAVOJOA, SONORA (BY TRAIN)

Gótzsche's September 27 letter to Merrild: "Monday we leave from here." (MER, 332)

OCTOBER 3–[2ND ALSO?] 4. AT MINAS NUEVAS, NEAR ALAMOS, SONORA

K. G. Gótzsche's October 4 letter to Merrild: "We have just come down from the Swiss' silver mine where we have been for a couple of days." (MER, 334) Lawrence's letter to Merrild on the following day: "We are still grilling in the sun of Navojoa. We came down yesterday from Minas Nuevas, over a road *much* worse than any Del Monte roads, and forty miles of it." (AH, 586) Lawrence's letter to Bynner, also October 5, also mentions the forty-mile Alamos road. (AH, 587) Gótzsche's October 15 letter to Merrild makes it clear that he and Lawrence went to Navojoa before making the side trip into the mountains. (MER, 336)

OCTOBER 5. LEAVE NAVOJOA FOR MAZATLÁN (BY TRAIN)

October 5 letter: "We are going on today to Mazatlán." (AH, 586)

OCTOBER 6 OR 7. ARRIVE AT MAZATLÁN, SINALOA

Lawrence dates a letter from there as October 6: "This is Sunday"—it was Saturday. (MER, 335)

BY OCTOBER 13. AT TEPIC, NAYARIT

Lawrence's letter of that date from Tepic: "We set off in the morning over the mountains . . . for Txlan [Etzatlán]: on Monday [the 15th] horseback all day, to pick up the other end of the railway. We should be in Guadalajara on Tuesday." (MER, 336)

OCTOBER 14. LEAVE TEPIC

(MER, 336)

ABOUT OCTOBER 16. ARRIVE AT GUADALAJARA, JALISCO (HOTEL GARCÍA)

Lawrence's letter from Guadalajara, dated October 17: "I got your letter here today—when I arrived from Tepic." (ML, 118) This conflicts with Gótzsche's Guadalajara letter to Merrild, dated October 15: "Today, at noon, we arrived in Guadalajara at last." (MER, 336) Perhaps each of the weary travelers was a day off in his dating. Elsewhere Lawrence also places the arrival on the 17th. (BR, 73)

OCTOBER 21. VISIT TO CHAPALA

Gótzsche's letter to Merrild, October 22: "Yesterday we were at Japala." (MER, 339)

NOVEMBER 17. LEAVE GUADALAJARA FOR MEXICO CITY (HOTEL MONTE CARLO)

"We got here this morning." (AH, 592)

NOVEMBER 22. LEAVE VERA CRUZ FOR PLYMOUTH, ABOARD THE *Toledo* (HAMBURG-AMERICAN LINE)

"We sail . . . on Thursday"—the 22nd. (AH, 593)

"I am sailing on the 22nd." (ML, 121)

NOVEMBER 25. AT HAVANA

Postcard to Knud Merrild: "Two days here." (MER, 351)

BY DECEMBER 7. IN LONDON (110 HEATH STREET, HAMPSTEAD)

"Here I am—in London." (AH, 597)

BY DECEMBER 31. AT NOTTINGHAM

Unpublished postcard to Frederick Carter places Lawrence there, though he was in London as late as the 27th, "due to go to the Midlands to my people." (ML, 132)

1924

The Lawrences become property owners when Mrs. Mabel Dodge Luhan of Taos presents Frieda with a ranch in the Sangre de Cristo mountains—the Flying Heart ranch, whose name Lawrence changes to Lobo and, later, to Kiowa. In August, *The Boy in the Bush* is published, as by D. H. Lawrence and M. L. Skinner. A book published in London in September—*Memoirs of the Foreign Legion*, by M.M.—contains an introduction by Lawrence, who

presents a memoir of the author of the book, the late
Maurice Magnus. Norman Douglas thereupon at-
tacks Lawrence and defends Magnus in a lively
pamphlet, *D. H. Lawrence and Maurice Magnus: A
Plea For Better Manners.*

JANUARY 3. TO PONTESBURY, SHROPSHIRE
    Unpublished letter to Frederick Carter, from Notting-
ham, January 1: "I shall leave Derby on Thursday morning
at 9.5, Great Northern Ry, get to Stafford 10.55, and to
Shrewsbury somewhere near midday."

JANUARY 5. BACK IN LONDON (110 HEATH STREET,
HAMPSTEAD)
    Unpublished letter to Carter, "Sunday" [January 6]:
"Got back here very nicely yesterday evening."

JANUARY 23. ARRIVE IN PARIS (HÔTEL VERSAILLES, 60
BOULEVARD MONTPARNASSE)
    January 24 postcard: "Came here yesterday." (MER,
356)

FEBRUARY 5. LEAVE PARIS
    Unpublished letter to Catherine Carswell, February 4:
"We go in the morning to Strasbourg."

FEBRUARY 7. ARRIVE BADEN-BADEN (C/O LUDWIG-
WILHELMSTIFT)
    "We've just got here." (AH, 601)

FEBRUARY 20. LEAVE BADEN-BADEN
    "We leave here on the 20th for Paris." (AH, 603)

FEBRUARY 21. ARRIVE IN PARIS (HÔTEL VERSAILLES)
    Unpublished letter to Catherine Carswell: "Just got
back here."

FEBRUARY 26. IN LONDON (GARLAND'S HOTEL, SUF-
FOLK STREET, PALL MALL)

Undated Paris letter to Curtis Brown: "I shall come to
London on Tuesday"—February 26. (AH, 604)

MARCH 5. SAIL ON *Aquitania* FOR NEW YORK

Diary entry March 5: "Left London for New York."
(LDN)

MARCH 11. ARRIVE NEW YORK

(AH, 605)

MARCH 18. LEAVE FOR CHICAGO

Letter to Catherine Carswell, March 16: "We're going
west on Tuesday morning [March 18]." (HM, 328)

MARCH 19. IN CHICAGO

Letter to Harriet Monroe from New York, March 12,
says, "I think we shall be going through to Taos on Tuesday
or Wednesday" and suggests seeing her between trains in
Chicago. Harriet Monroe recalled the Lawrences and a
friend spending a day in what he called the "queer big
city" (*Poetry: A Magazine of Verse*, May, 1930). Further
references, by Lawrence, to that visit are in AH, 606 and 716.

MARCH 21. ARRIVE AT SANTA FE

"On March 21, 1924, I wrote my mother from Santa Fe
that they 'came at six this evening. . . . They go along to
Taos tomorrow.'" (BYN, 247)

MARCH 22. ARRIVE AT TAOS (MRS. LUHAN'S HOUSE)

Resides at Taos until May 5.

APRIL 23. AT SANTA FE

Unpublished postcard to Catherine Carswell, April 23: "We came down here for a day or two, to Indian dances." Unpublished postcard to Mark Gertler, apparently of same date (postmark blurred): "We came down here for a few days, for the Indian dances."

MAY 5. TO LOBO RANCH, NEAR QUESTA

Diary entry May 5: "Went to Lobo from Taos, to build up the ranch." (LDN, 98)

Resides at Lobo until October 11.

AUGUST 14. AT SANTA FE

Postcard to Else Jaffe (FR, 170), as well as unpublished postcards to Catherine Carswell and Mark Gertler from Santa Fe on this day, speak of going to the Indian dances; Gertler's card, which mentions the time the journey will take, says, "We are motoring about ten days to the Hopi Country."

ABOUT AUGUST 15. AT NEW LAGUNA, VALENCIA COUNTY, NEW MEXICO

"We slept at a small adobe inn at New Laguna." (ML, 257)

ABOUT AUGUST 16. AT ST. MICHAEL'S, APACHE RESERVATION, ARIZONA; AND TO MISHONGHOVI, HOPI RESERVATION, ARIZONA

"By noon time" at St. Michael's. (ML, 259) "I know we came to Mishonghovi, and we camped below the great rock mesa that was capped, on its summit, with the Hopi village." (ML, 266)

AUGUST 17. TO HOTEVILLA, HOPI INDIAN RESERVATION

"On the Sunday afternoon of August 17th . . . to Hotevilla, where the dance is." (MIM, 136, 137)

AUGUST 18. AT HOTEVILLA

"Afternoon of the next day," the Lawrence party is still there. (MIM, 161)

ABOUT AUGUST 18 OR 19. AT MONTEZUMA CASTLE, NEAR CAMP VERDE, YAVAPAI COUNTY, ARIZONA

"After the Snake Dance ceremonial we motored to the Canyon de Chelly, because I thought Lorenzo would like to see Montezuma's White House." (ML, 266)

ABOUT AUGUST 21. BACK TO SANTA FE

Apparently the trip lasted several days more, with a camp one night "on the summit of the Continental Divide." The party eventually returned to Santa Fe, and the Lawrences left, after perhaps one night, for Taos. (ML, 267, 268)

AUGUST 22. AT TAOS (MRS. LUHAN'S)

Lawrence's undated letter to Mrs. Luhan in Santa Fe speaks of "tomorrow morning—Sunday"; hence it was written on Saturday the 23rd; and it suggests the Lawrences had arrived the day before. (ML, 268)

AUGUST 24. BACK TO LOBO RANCH (RENAMED KIOWA RANCH)

Lawrence's letter of August 23: "I think I shall go up tomorrow morning—Sunday." (ML, 268)

OCTOBER 11. LEAVE KIOWA RANCH FOR TAOS (EN ROUTE TO MEXICO)

Diary entry October 10: "Leave tomorrow." (LDN, 99)

OCTOBER 11–[?]13. AT TAOS

"We shall go down to Taos on Saturday [11th], stay a day or two, then go down to Mexico City." (AH, 625) "Lorenzo and Frieda came down and passed a few days here [in Taos] before they left for Mexico." (ML, 277)

? OCTOBER 13–19?. AT SANTA FE

Undated Lawrence letter to Mrs. Luhan suggests Friday, October 17. It refers to Bynner's expected arrival on "Saturday" and Lawrence's hope to get away "today—if not, we shall have to stay till Sunday, as we'd get no Visas if we arrived El Paso Sunday." (ML, 279) He apparently stayed until Sunday.

OCTOBER 20. IN EL PASO (LEAVING FOR MEXICO)

Unpublished postcard to Catherine Carswell, October 20: "We cross into Mexico this morning."

OCTOBER 23. ARRIVE AT MEXICO CITY (HOTEL MONTE CARLO, AVENIDA URUGUAY)

"Friday" [24th] letter: "We got here after midnight on Wed." (AH, 627)

NOVEMBER 8. TO OAXACA

Diary entry November 8: "Leave Mexico City for Oaxaca." (LDN, 99)

NOVEMBER 9. ARRIVE AT OAXACA (HOTEL FRANCIA)

"We got down here Sunday night [9th]: it takes two days from Mexico City." (HM, 334) The "arrived yesterday" diary entry is evidently dated incorrectly (as the 11th). (LDN, 99)

NOVEMBER 18. TO AVENIDA PINO SUAREZ 43, OAXACA

Diary entry November 17: "Move into Richards house tomorrow." (LDN, 99)

Resides at Avenida Pino Suarez 43 until February 14, 1925.

1925

At Oaxaca, Mexico, in February, Lawrence completes *The Plumed Serpent* and collapses into an illness that nearly proves fatal. In May, Lawrence's short novel *St. Mawr* is published in London. The New York edition, which follows soon after, omits the long story "The Princess," which the English volume includes. In December, after Lawrence's return to Europe, a Philadelphia bookshop issues a limited edition of his essays, *Reflections on the Death of a Porcupine*.

FEBRUARY 14. TO HOTEL FRANCIA?—OAXACA

February 14 letter: "Am still in Oaxaca—but was moved down to this hotel yesterday." (AH, 637) The letter probably was on stationery which identified "this hotel," which may have once again been the Francia.

BY MARCH 2. IN MEXICO CITY (HOTEL IMPERIAL)

March 2d letter shows Lawrence there. (AH, 638) In a March 3 letter, he says, "We struggled up here last week." (BYN, 252)

? MARCH 23 OR 24?. LEAVE MEXICO CITY FOR EL PASO, TEXAS

Unpublished letter to A. D. Hawk, March 19: "We shall

leave on Monday for El Paso, or at latest, on Tuesday: that is the 24th. So we should be in Santa Fe by 27th."

ABOUT MARCH 26–28. AT EL PASO

Lawrence, telling Amy Lowell of his difficulties in getting back across the American border, says, "After two days' fight we got through." (SFD, 697; HM, 340)

MARCH 29. ARRIVE AT SANTA FE (DE VARGAS HOTEL)

Unpublished letter to A. D. Hawk, dated only "Sunday," says: "We got here this afternoon."

APRIL 1. TO DEL MONTE RANCH (VISITING THE HAWKS)

April 2 letter: "We got here yesterday. . . . We're staying with our neighbors for a while." (HM, 339)

APRIL 5. TO KIOWA RANCH

Letter to Amy Lowell, April 6: "—and yesterday got to our little ranch." (SFD, 697; HM, 340)

SEPTEMBER 10. LEAVE KIOWA RANCH FOR NEW YORK AND ENGLAND

"We leave here Sept. 10th—expect to be in England by first week in October." (HM, 343)

ABOUT SEPTEMBER 14. ARRIVE AT NEW YORK (71 WASHINGTON PLACE)

"I didn't care much for New York, the eight days we were there this time." (ML, 289) Since he left on the 22nd, he perhaps arrived about the 14th.

SEPTEMBER 22. LEAVE FOR EUROPE (S.S. *Resolute*)

Unpublished letter to Mrs. Bessie Freeman, September 21: "We sail tonight"; but in a shipboard letter of September 27, Lawrence says, "We went on board last Monday night [21st], and sailed at 1 a. m." (HM, 344)

SEPTEMBER 30. ARRIVE AT SOUTHAMPTON, HAMP-SHIRE; ON TO LONDON

"We get to Southampton on Wednesday morning"—the 30th. (HM, 343) Mrs. Carswell remembered that "the Lawrences arrived as planned, and went first to Garland's Hotel [Suffolk Street, Pall Mall]." (CC, 227) That the Lawrences had taken the train directly to London is shown by Murry's reference: "On 1st October I was surprised to have a postcard [unpublished] from him saying he had arrived in London the night before." (RMM, 112)

OCTOBER 7. TO NOTTINGHAMSHIRE AND DERBYSHIRE

"We are going today up to the Midlands, to stay with my sisters." (HM, 345) Catherine Carswell says that Lawrence, traveling alone, spent "a day or a night" with the Carswells at High Wycombe, possibly about October 8–9, though Mrs. Carswell, perhaps through a slip of memory, placed Lawrence there on a Sunday—the 8th and 9th were a Thursday and Friday. (CC, 227)

OCTOBER 14. TO RIPLEY, DERBYSHIRE (C/O MRS. W. E. CLARKE, GEE STREET)

Unpublished letter to Mrs. Carswell, dated "Tuesday" [13th]: "We are going to Ripley tomorrow"—indicating that he had been staying in Eastwood or elsewhere in the Midlands: "The weather's awful, and we simply hate it up here."

ABOUT OCTOBER 22. TO LONDON (73 GOWER STREET)

Unpublished letter to Gordon Macfarlane, dated from Ripley on a "Friday" or October 16: "I don't think we shall get to London till Wednesday or even Thursday." An unpublished "Saturday" letter to Mrs. Carswell: "We think of staying here till Wed.—or even Thursday."

OCTOBER 29. LEAVE LONDON FOR BADEN-BADEN
"We leave for Baden-Baden on Thursday"—October 29. (BR, 83) This letter, written on October 26, a Monday, makes it possible to date the "Monday" letter to J. M. Murry: "We leave for Baden-Baden on Thursday." (AH, 648)

BY OCTOBER 31. AT BADEN-BADEN (HOTEL EDEN)
(AH, 649)

NOVEMBER 15. ARRIVE AT SPOTORNO, RIVIERA PO-NENTE, ITALY (VILLA MARIA)
November 16 letter: "We got here yesterday." (AH, 649)

BY NOVEMBER 19. AT VILLA BERNARDA, SPOTORNO
"We've taken a house here till April." (AH, 650)

Resides at Villa Bernarda until April 20, 1926.

1926

The first edition of *The Plumed Serpent* appears in London in January. In February, "weary of being slandered," Lawrence strikes back at Douglas in the columns of the *New Statesman,* several months after Douglas has reprinted his Magnus-Lawrence essay in his book *Experiments.* In October, at the Villa Mirenda near Florence, Lawrence begins writing his novel *Lady Chatterley's Lover.* Also during that autumn, Lawrence, who has been mildly interested in the activity most of his life, begins painting pictures consistently.

FEBRUARY 22. LEAVE SPOTORNO FOR MONTE CARLO, MONACO

"I'm going away with my sister on Monday [22nd] for a few days." (HM, 351)

FEBRUARY 24. AT MONTE CARLO

"Staying here for a few days." (HM, 351)

ABOUT MARCH 2. AT CAPRI (VILLA QUATRO VENTI)

Letter from Frieda Lawrence to Mabel Luhan, March 2: "Lawrence is in Capri." (ML, 291)

MARCH 18. AT RAVELLO, PROVÍNCIA DI SALERNO, ITALY

March 18 letter from Ravello: "I have been moving around." (ML, 291) Later, Lawrence wrote the Brewsters, after his return to Spotorno, April 11: "I stayed ten days or so in Ravello—very nice. . . . Then with my friends I came slowly north, staying in Rome, Perugia, Assisi, Florence, Ravenna—and so here." (BR, 94)

APRIL 3. RETURN TO VILLA BERNARDA, SPOTORNO

Letter of "Easter Sunday" [April 4] from Spotorno: "I arrived yesterday." (FR, 183) Letter of "Easter Monday": "I got back here day before yesterday—wandered around seeing friends for six weeks." (AH, 662) Letter to Else Jaffe-Richthofen, incorrectly dated as *March 7:* "I got back here on Saturday." (FR, 184)

APRIL 20. TO FLORENCE (PENSIONE LUCCHESI, LUNGARNO ZECCA)

April 19 letter: "We leave here tomorrow." (ML, 297) April 19 letter: "We leave for Florence tomorrow." (ALC, 108) April 24 letter: "We left Spotorno last Tuesday"—

April 20. (HM, 353) The statement in a letter from Florence dated April 25—"We came here last Thursday"—must be wrong. (BR, 95) April 20 was a Tuesday.

ABOUT MAY 13. MOVE TO VILLA MIRENDA, SAN PAOLO MOSCIANO, SCANDICCI, FLORENCE

First authenticated, available letter from Villa Mirenda is of this date. (AH, 666) Last from Florence (Pensione Lucchesi) is of May 3. (ALC, 108) The move to the Mirenda, not mentioned in that letter, may have been made on the 13th or shortly before, since Lawrence did not mention it to his most familiar correspondents until some days later. Earl Brewster, for example, was not told of it until a letter of May 17 (BR, 98), and Catherine Carswell not until a letter of May 18 (unpublished). Attempts to date the Lawrences' move to Villa Mirenda are complicated by a letter dated May 8 from there (ML, 299), but this was certainly written on June 8, for on May 17 Lawrence wrote Mrs. Luhan from there as if for the first time, describing the new home (ML, 301); also, the wrongly dated "May" 8 letter refers to the arrival of Dorothy Brett in the United States—she did not sail until May 2, from Naples, and was not expecting to reach America until May 16. On June 8 Lawrence also misdated a letter to a less frequent correspondent: an unpublished letter of that date to John Cournos, also written from the Mirenda ("I told you, didn't I, we'd taken half this villa for a year"), is likewise misdated *May* 8—the same kind of error as in the letter to Else Jaffe-Richthofen referred to under the April 3 entry, above.

Resides—intermittently—at Villa Mirenda until June 10, 1928.

JULY 12. LEAVE FLORENCE FOR BADEN-BADEN, VIA MILAN

"We leave here next Monday—the 12th." (AH, 673)

JULY 13. ARRIVE AT BADEN-BADEN (C/O FRAU VON RICHTHOFEN, LUDWIG-WILHELMSTIFT)

"We leave next Monday the twelfth for Milan, and on Tuesday the thirteenth from Milan to Baden-Baden. We arrive at 6.45 in the evening." (FR, 250)

JULY 29. LEAVE BADEN-BADEN FOR LONDON

Letter of that date: "We leave tonight, via Strasbourg, Brussels, Ostend, for London: through the night." (AH, 675)

JULY 31. ARRIVE AT LONDON (25 ROSSETTI MANSIONS, FLOOD STREET, CHELSEA)

Evident from the foregoing.

BY AUGUST 8. IN SCOTLAND ("BAILABHADAN," NEW-TONMORE, INVERNESS-SHIRE)

Letter of this date from Frieda Lawrence: "Lawrence is in Scotland." (ML, 307) Between July 31 and Lawrence's departure for Scotland, he spent a few days with Richard Aldington at Malthouse Cottage, Padworth, Berkshire; this is the visit Aldington mentioned in *Life for Life's Sake*, though it can hardly have been the "long weekend" he refers to (p. 301) because the Lawrences did not arrive in London until a Saturday—the 31st of July—and Lawrence was in Scotland by the next Sunday, August 8. The visit took place in the first week of August; in the August 8 letter, Frieda Lawrence says, "Then we went to see the Richard Aldingtons." During Lawrence's fortnight in Scotland, he went on "an excursion to the west, to Fort William and Maillag, and sailed up from Maillag to the Isle of Skye." (FR, 212)

AUGUST 21. LEAVE SCOTLAND

August 20 letter: "I am going south, tomorrow, to stay with my sisters in Lincolnshire for a little while, by the sea." (FR, 212)

ABOUT AUGUST 22–23. AT MABLETHORPE, LINCOLN-SHIRE

August 26 letter: "I've been here a few days." (AH, 676)

BY AUGUST 29. AT SUTTON-ON-SEA, LINCOLNSHIRE ("DUNEVILLE," TRUSTHORPE ROAD)

(BR, 103)

SEPTEMBER 13. LEAVE SUTTON-ON-SEA

"We leave here tomorrow." (AH, 677)

SEPTEMBER 16. ARRIVE AT LONDON (CARLINGFORD HOUSE, 30 WILLOUGHBY ROAD, HAMPSTEAD)

Letter of Monday, September 12: "By Thursday I expect to be in London." (AH, 677) This phrase also occurs in an unpublished letter to Orioli, September 11.

SEPTEMBER 28. LEAVE LONDON FOR FLORENCE

September 23 letter: "We leave here on Tuesday [28th], and stay a few days in Paris, on our way to Florence." (ML, 310)

ABOUT SEPTEMBER 28–OCTOBER 3. AT PARIS?

Suggested by the foregoing and by an unpublished letter to Millicent Beveridge from Sutton-on-Sea on "Saturday" [11th]: "Probably we shall stay in Paris a few days, in the littré, on our way out."

OCTOBER 4. ARRIVE AT VILLA MIRENDA, SCANDICCI, FLORENCE

"Last night, the rooms being only just opened, it was so hot I could not sleep"—statement in October 5 letter, indicating arrival on previous day. (ALC, 109)

Resides at Villa Mirenda until March 18, 1927.

1927

In a year in which only one of his books is published —*Mornings in Mexico,* in July—Lawrence continues to write *Lady Chatterley's Lover.* In the early spring, he tours the Etruscan cities and afterward writes his essays about them, published as magazine articles and collected after his death into one of his most important travel books, *Etruscan Places* (1932).

MARCH 18. TO ROME

Unpublished letter to Enid Hilton, March 17: "I am going to Rome tomorrow, then south to Ravello."

ABOUT MARCH 20. LEAVE ROME

April 14 letter, after return to Villa Mirenda: "I stayed two nights in Christine Hughes' flat in Rome." (ML, 326) This visit may have been a few weeks later, when Lawrence came back through Rome with Earl Brewster; but the probabilities favor March 18–20. The visit is described in the "Laura Philippine" essay in *Assorted Articles,* which mentions an automobile trip to Ostia.

BY MARCH 22. AT RAVELLO, PROVÍNCIA DI SALERNO (PALAZZO CIMBRONE, "ABOVE AMALFI")

(AH, 690)

ABOUT MARCH 28. LEAVE RAVELLO

"I shall probably start on a little walking tour next week—the 28th—walking north." (AH, 690) Earl Brewster remembered, "One day, after the promised visit to us in Ravello, Lawrence and I drove out to the end of the Sorrentine Peninsula, returning to Sorrento on foot. . . . From Sorrento we started on our Etruscan pilgrimage, beginning with the museum of the Villa di Papa Giulia in Rome." (EB, 120, 122)

APRIL 6. FROM ROME TO CERVETERI AND CIVITAVÉCCHIA, PROVÍNCIA DI ROMA

Date may be deduced from end date (established) of Etruscan tour. *Etruscan Places* describes departure from Rome on morning train and arrival at Palo; arrival at Cerveteri; arrival at hotel in Civitavecchia. (EP, 13, 14, 46)

APRIL 7. ARRIVE AT TARQUINIA (GENTILE'S INN)

Same book describes arrival in Tarquinia on following day; describes departure two days later. (EP, 48, 141)

APRIL 9. TO MONTALTO DI CASTRO AND VOLCI (FORMERLY VULCI)

"We took the train, one station only [beyond Tarquinia], to Montalto di Castro. . . . The morning was still fairly early—and Saturday." (EP, 141, 142) "The drive to the Ponte [at Volci] was approximately two hours—then the trip would be six hours." (EP, 143) "The café man asked if we would stay the night [at Montalto, after returning from Volci] . . . I decided that, if we could, we would leave in the evening." (EP, 145) Apparently Lawrence went on that evening to Grosseto, not mentioned in *Etruscan Places;* in a letter of April 14, Lawrence mentions visiting Grosseto between Vulci and Volterra (FR, 223); and mentions his arrival at Volterra on a Sunday afternoon, or April 10. (EP, 174) Earl Brewster remembered, "that Easter morning found us in Grosseto" (BR, 123); but this was Palm Sunday, April 10.

APRIL 10. TO VOLTERRA

From the foregoing, and from *Etruscan Places:* "You leave the Rome–Pisa train [which runs through Grosseto] at Cecina, and slowly wind up the valley . . . to a stop at the Saline di Volterra. . . . and are rattled up to the final level of the city." (EP, 173, 174)

APRIL 11. RETURN TO FLORENCE (VILLA MIRENDA, SCANDICCI)

Earl Brewster recalled: "At Volterra our Etruscan pilgrimage ended. Lawrence climbed into the great-motor-bus for Florence." (BR, 124) Also, Lawrence in an April 14 letter from Villa Mirenda said: "I got home all right Monday night—pretty well shaken up, after five hours in that bus." (BR, 124)

MID-JUNE. AT FORTE DEI MARMI. PROVÍNCIA DI LUCCA

June 21 letter from Villa Mirenda: "We too were away at the seaside, about a hundred miles from here, not far, a place called Forte dei Marmi. Maria Huxley motored us down. . . ." (ALC, 126) Undated letter to Earl Brewster: "We motored home via Lucca." (BR, 138)

AUGUST 4. LEAVE FLORENCE FOR VILLACH, AUSTRIA

August 3 letter from Villa Mirenda: "We're going to Austria tomorrow, D. V." (AH, 697) An unpublished letter to G. Orioli, "Thursday night August 4, 1927": "Well here we are at your flat"—apparently waiting for the night train.

August 8 letter from Villach: "Well here we are—got
through on Thursday night in the *wagon-lit*." (AH, 697)

AUGUST 5. AT VILLACH, KÄRNTEN, AUSTRIA (HOTEL
FISCHER)
     From above: "We got here on Friday"—the 5th. (BR,
143)

AUGUST 29. LEAVE VILLACH FOR SALZBURG
     Unpublished postcard to G. Orioli, from Villach, Au-
gust 24: "We leave here next Monday—29th—for Salzburg."

AUGUST 31. IRSCHENHAUSEN, BAVARIA (VILLA JAFFE)
     Postcard of September 4: "We came here on Wed. eve-
ning"—31st. (ALC, 131)

OCTOBER 4. TO BADEN-BADEN (HOTEL EDEN)
     Letter of September 29: "Wait then till Tuesday [Octo-
ber 4], when we are coming. We take the twelve o'clock
train and arrive at seven in Baden, is that right, mother-in-
law?" (FR, 233)

ABOUT OCTOBER 18. LEAVE BADEN-BADEN
     Unpublished letter to G. Orioli, dated only "Wed." but
obviously written on the 12th: "We want to leave here next
Tuesday—so we ought to arrive in Florence on Wednesday
evening—19th from Milan."

OCTOBER 20. ARRIVE AT VILLA MIRENDA, SCANDICCI,
FLORENCE
     October 21 letter: "We got back here yesterday." (BR,
150)

1928

In January, Lawrence completes the third and final version of *Lady Chatterley's Lover*, and supervises arrangements for its publication by subscription. By April the orders are sufficient to pay for the first edition, and by July copies begin to circulate. Meanwhile, Lawrence's short-story collection, *The Woman Who Rode Away*, is published in London on May 24 and, in a somewhat different version, in New York on the following day. In September, *The Collected Poems of D. H. Lawrence*, in two volumes, make their first appearance in London.

JANUARY 18 OR 19. LEAVE FOR LES DIABLERETS, VAUD, SWITZERLAND

January 17 letter: "I hope we shall get off on Wed. or Thursday"—the 18th or 19th. (AH, 708)

ABOUT JANUARY 21. AT LES DIABLERETS (CHÂLET BEAU SITE)

"I hope we shall . . . be in Diablerets anyhow on Saturday"—the 21st. (AH, 708)

MARCH 6. LEAVE FOR MILAN, VIA SWITZERLAND AND DOMODOSSOLA

March 4 letter: "We leave here—at least I do, for Frieda is already in Baden-Baden—on Tuesday [6th]. We meet in Milan and ought to be in the Villa Mirenda on Wednesday evening." (AH, 713)

MARCH 7. ARRIVE AT VILLA MIRENDA, SCANDICCI, FLORENCE

Undated "Wednesday" letter should be dated March 7; it says, "We have just entered the Villa Mirenda." (FR,

222) March 8 letter: "Got home all right last night." (AH, 714)

JUNE 10. LEAVE FLORENCE FOR SWITZERLAND

Unpublished "Thursday" letter to G. Orioli, obviously written on June 8: "We want to go Sunday [10th] at about midday—by Pisa-Genoa-Turin." Letter of June 7: "We are leaving on Sunday, for the French Alps." (MXR, 31)

JUNE 11. LEAVE TURIN FOR CHAMBÉRY, SAVOIE, FRANCE

Mrs. Brewster remembered that on the day she and her husband went north with the Lawrences, "when we reached Turin . . . we decided to spend the night." (BR, 282) "Our next stop was Chambéry." (BR, 283)

ABOUT JUNE 13–17. AT CHAMBÉRY AND AIX-LES-BAINS, SAVOIE, AND GRENOBLE AND ST.-NIZIER, ISÈRE

Mrs. Brewster mentions the hotel at Aix-les-Bains, and then: "From Grenoble we motored up . . . to . . . St. Nizier-de-Pariset, and . . . on the following day we returned . . . to settle in," but after one night there "we went at once to a familiar hotel in Chexbres-sur-Vevey." (BR, 283, 284, 285)

JUNE 17. ARRIVE AT CHEXBRES-SUR-VEVEY, VAUD, SWITZERLAND (GRAND HOTEL)

Unpublished postcard to Catherine Carswell, postmarked June 22: "We got here Sunday"—the 17th.

JUNE 27. SPEND THE DAY AT CHILLON AND MONTREUX

Unpublished letter to G. Orioli, June 28: "We motored to Chillon yesterday—and had tea in Montreux."

JULY 6. TO GSTAAD, BERN, SWITZERLAND (HOTEL NATIONAL)

Unpublished letter to G. Orioli, July 4: "We leave here Friday [6th] to look for a place higher up." "Sunday evening" letter to Earl Brewster from Hotel National, Gstaad: "We have decided to go out to the châlet tomorrow, Monday evening, at six o'clock—it saves another day at this dull hotel." (BR, 172)

JULY 9. TO GSTEIG BEI GSTAAD, BERN, SWITZERLAND (CHÂLET KESSELMATTE)

Unpublished "Monday" postcard to Enid Hilton, postmarked July 10: "Well we've . . . got a little peasant châlet here. . . . We only came in at teatime, now it's nightfall."

Resides at Gsteig until September 18.

AUGUST 10. SPEND THE DAY AT LES DIABLERETS

Unpublished letter to G. Orioli, August 10: "We went to Diablerets today."

SEPTEMBER 18. LEAVE GSTEIG FOR BADEN-BADEN (HOTEL LÖWEN, LICHTENTHAL)

September 12 letter: "We leave here next Monday 17th." (HM, 388). This plan was changed, according to an unpublished "Sunday" [16th] letter to G. Orioli: "We are not leaving till Tuesday." September 22 letter from Baden-Baden: "We are here since Tuesday [18th]." (AH, 761) Unpublished letter, same date and place, to G. Orioli: "We got here all right Tuesday night."

OCTOBER 1. LEAVE BADEN-BADEN FOR HYÈRES, VAR, FRANCE

Unpublished letter from Baden-Baden to Harry Crosby, September 30: "I am leaving here tomorrow—going Strasbourg-Lyon direct, so shan't come through Paris." Unpublished letter, same date and place, to G. Orioli: "I am leaving tomorrow morning for Hyères, near Toulon."

OCTOBER 2–15. "ON THAT BIT OF RIVIERA NEAR HYÈRES," CHIEFLY AT LA LAVANDOU, VAR

September 25 letter: "I shall go on Tuesday to S. of France. . . . F.'s sister Else is down just [sic] there till 8th Oct. So I'll try it—and Frieda can join me somewhere there . . . on that bit of Riviera near Hyères." (AH, 763) "Lawrence would not come to the island [Port-Cros] without Frieda, and he waited for her at Le Lavandou with his sister[-in-law], and, part of the time, with the Huxleys. . . . The Lawrences did not reach Port-Cros until about two weeks after the original rendezvous." (RA, 394) Lawrence's stay at Le Lavandou is recorded on a postcard to his sister (ALC, 142–143), and on three cards to the Brewsters (BR, 181–182), one of which describes a visit to Port-Cros by motorboat: "The Vigie—fortress—is an hour's stony walk uphill. . . . Tomorrow the Aldingtons come and I decide if we shall stay at the Vigie for two months."

OCTOBER 15. TO ÎLE DE PORT-CROS, VAR (LA VIGIE)

"Saturday" letter, obviously October 13: "F. joined me last night from Florence—on Monday we go over to the island." Unpublished letter to Mrs. Enid Hilton, October 21: "We came here last Monday."

NOVEMBER 17. TO BANDOL, VAR (HÔTEL BEAU RIVAGE)

"Sunday" letter from Bandol: "We got here yesterday,

quite nice; beastly crossing from that island." (BR, 185)
The date of departure from Port-Cros and arrival at Bandol
was Saturday, November 17. Lawrence was still at Port-
Cros on November 14 (AH, 769); and was settled in Bandol by the 24th. (AH, 771)

Resides at Bandol until March 11, 1929

1929

British government officials seize the manuscript
copies of Lawrence's *Pansies* poems as they come
through the mails, registered, from southern France.
Lawrence's London publisher issues *Pansies* in July
with fourteen of the poems missing, but a privately
printed "special definitive edition" a month later includes them. Meanwhile, an unexpurgated "popular"
edition of *Lady Chatterley* has appeared in Paris
with Lawrence's prefatory account of his struggles
with book pirates: "My Skirmish With Jolly Roger."
In London, in June, reproductions of twenty-eight
of his pictures appear in color in *The Paintings of
D. H. Lawrence*. At this time his exhibition of paintings opens; on July 5, policemen carry away thirteen
of the paintings. A magistrate permits them to be
returned to Lawrence, then in Italy, with the understanding that they will not be exhibited publicly
again. In September, the Black Sun Press in Paris
brings out Lawrence's last important work of fiction,
The Escaped Cock, timidly known in all subsequent
reprints as *The Man Who Died*. In November, Lawrence's pamphlet *Pornography and Obscenity* is one
of the successes of the season. Lawrence during
1929 writes some of his finest poetry, first published
in Florence in 1932 in *Last Poems*.

MARCH 11. LEAVE BANDOL FOR PARIS (HÔTEL DE VER-
SAILLES, 60 BOULEVARD MONTPARNASSE)

March 10 letter: "We leave in the morning." (HM,

402) Undated letter to the Huxleys: "expect to arrive Paris at 10.0 on Tuesday night" (AH, 797); later plans apparently changed this to Monday night, the 11th.

BY MARCH 18. AT SURESNES, SEINE (3 RUE DE BAC)

Unpublished letter to G. Orioli, March 18: "I am staying with Aldous and Maria [Huxley] for a few days."

MARCH 25. RETURN TO PARIS (HÔTEL DE VERSAILLES)

Unpublished letter to Orioli, March 26: "I came back here yesterday, and Frieda arrived last night."

ABOUT MARCH 30–31. AT ERMENONVILLE, OISE, FRANCE (LE MOULIN DE SOLEIL)

"In spring D. H. Lawrence and Frieda, his wife, came to visit us at our 'Moulin du Soleil.'" (TPY, 222) Mrs. Crosby remembers this as "that weekend," and since the March 30–31 weekend was the only one at that time during which Frieda Lawrence was in the Paris area, the visit probably took place then.

APRIL 7. LEAVE PARIS FOR PERPIGNAN, BARCELONA, AND PALMA DE MAJORCA

April 6 letter: "We leave in the morning—via Orléans and Toulouse." (AH, 801) "Tomorrow we leave, going south to Lyon, Avignon, Perpignan, and so to Spain." (MXR, 34)

APRIL 10. AT CARCASSONNE, AUDE, FRANCE (HÔTEL DE LA CITÉ)

Unpublished letter from this place, to Charles Lahr, April 10: "Tomorrow I hope we shall get to Perpignan."

ABOUT APRIL 11. AT PERPIGNAN, PYRÉNÉES ORIENTALES, FRANCE

Evident from the foregoing.

BY APRIL 15. AT BARCELONA

"We have got so far—and tomorrow night we cross to Palma, Majorca." (BR, 200)

APRIL 17. TO PALMA DE MAJORCA, BALEARES (HOTEL ROYAL, THEN HOTEL PRÍNCIPE ALFONSO)

April 27 letter: "We have been here ten days." (AH, 803) The date is also suggested by the statement in the April 15 entry. On April 18 (in a letter incorrectly dated May 9 in HM, 403), Lawrence was at the Hotel Royal, describing the island in some detail to G. Orioli. By April 24 (in a letter incorrectly dated April 25 in AH, 801) Lawrence was writing to Rhys Davies from the Hotel Príncipe Alfonso.

JUNE 18. LEAVE MAJORCA FOR MARSEILLES

June 12 letter: "We intend to leave here definitely next Tuesday, the 18th, for Marseilles." (MXR, 166) June 23 letter from Italy: "We left Majorca last Tuesday." (AH, 815)

JUNE 22. ARRIVE AT FORTE DEI MARMI, LUCCA, ITALY (PENSIONE GIULIANI, VIALE MORIN)

Unpublished letter to Orioli, dated only "Sunday" but obviously written on June 23: "I got here last night—Frieda is in England." This "Sunday" letter is probably more reliable than the June 26 letter: "Ich bin hier seit Sonntag." (MXR, 167)

JULY 7. TO FLORENCE (6 LUNGARNO CORSINI)

July 2 letter: "I am going to Florence on Saturday"— the 7th. (MXR, 167) Unpublished postcard to G. Orioli, dated "Friday tea-time" and postmarked from Forte dei Marmi on July 6: "I shall arrive tomorrow evening, as I said, at 7.12 (19.12) by the quick train."

JULY 16. LEAVE FLORENCE FOR BADEN-BADEN

"Florence, Dienstag" letter: "So fahren wir heute Abend ab." (MXR, 169) And an unpublished letter to Charles Lahr ("Florence. Tuesday evening"): "We are off just now." This was Tuesday, July 16. A July 10 letter shows Lawrence planning to leave "Sunday or Monday," the 14th or 15th. (AH, 816)

ABOUT JULY 17. ARRIVE AT BADEN-BADEN (HOTEL LÖWEN, LICHTENTHAL)

Suggested by the foregoing: the journey seems to have been a direct one. Unpublished postcard to G. Orioli, dated "Saturday" and postmarked July 20: "We had quite an easy journey here." July 19 letters show the Lawrences already at Hotel Löwen. (ALC, 150 and BR, 204)

JULY 24. TO KURHAUS PLÄTTIG, BEI BÜHL, BADEN

July 20 letter: "My wife and her mother want us to go on Wednesday [24th] up to the Plättig—about 3,000 feet up—only an hour or so drive from here." (AH, 817) July 25 letter shows Lawrence established there. (AH, 818)

AUGUST 3. BACK TO BADEN-BADEN (HOTEL LÖWEN)

August 2 letter: "Tomorrow we are going down." (HM, 412)

AUGUST 25. TO MUNICH

August 24 letter: "We leave in the morning for Bavaria." (HM, 415) Letter to Max Mohr, August 22, is more specific: "Also wir reisen Sonntag um 10.28 Uhr ab und kommen um 17.55 Uhr an München . . . Wir bleiben die Nacht in München und kommen mit der Bahn an Tegernsee am Montag Morgen." (MXR, 172)

AUGUST 26. TO ROTTACH-AM-TEGERNSEE, BAVARIA
(KAFFEE ANGERMEIER)

The foregoing makes it evident that after spending the night of the 25th in Munich, the Lawrences went the next day to Rottach.

SEPTEMBER 18. LEAVE ROTTACH FOR SOUTH OF FRANCE

Unpublished letter from Rottach to Charles Lahr, September 16: "We leave here Wed. morning [18th], and I shall write from S. of France."

SEPTEMBER 23. ARRIVE AT BANDOL, VAR, FRANCE
(HÔTEL BEAU RIVAGE)

"We arrived Monday evening—three days ago." (BR, 219) This letter is misdated in the Brewsters' book as September 17; possibly Lawrence wrote it on the 27th which was a Friday. (See the discussion in Preface, p. x.) Unpublished letters of September 23 suggest by their brevity that they were written immediately after arrival; one, to Caresse Crosby, says "We are back at the winter address"; another, to Charles Lahr, says, "So glad to be back," and mentions a stop over in Marseilles.

Resides at Bandol until February 6, 1930.

OCTOBER 1. MOVE TO VILLA BEAU SOLEIL, BANDOL

Unpublished letter to Frederick Carter, October 1: "We have taken this house for six months, and are moving in today."

1930

In March, the month of Lawrence's death, his little volume of *Nettles*—poems to sting his censors and critics—comes out in London. In the following month, his *Assorted Articles,* some of his last essays, appears; and, in June, the expansion of his "Jolly Roger" essay as *A Propos of Lady Chatterley's Lover.* For the next several years, other Lawrence books will appear, the most notable of them being Aldous Huxley's edition of *The Letters of D. H. Lawrence* (1932).

Lawrence died on March 2 at Vence, Alpes Maritimes, France, and was buried, March 4, in the cemetery at Vence.

FEBRUARY 6. TO VENCE, ALPES MARITIMES (AD ASTRA SANATORIUM)

February 3 letter: "I have decided to go to the Sanatorium . . . on Thursday"—or February 6. (ALC, 157) Letter of "Friday," or February 7: "I came yesterday" to Vence. (AH, 858)

MARCH 1. MOVES TO VILLA ROBERMOND

"We are moving into a house here at Vence on Saturday"—March 1. (ALC, 158 and BR, 232)

MARCH 2. DEATH OF D. H. LAWRENCE AT VILLA ROBERMOND

"A telegram came saying: 'Lawrence died ten o'clock night of March second, funeral four o'clock March fourth.'" (BR, 310)